bash
Pocket Reference

bash
Pocket Reference

Arnold Robbins

O'REILLY®

Beijing · Cambridge · Farnham · Köln · Sebastopol · Tokyo

bash Pocket Reference
by Arnold Robbins

Copyright © 2010 Arnold Robbins. All rights reserved.
Printed in the United States of America.

Published by O'Reilly Media, Inc., 1005 Gravenstein Highway North, Sebastopol, CA 95472.

O'Reilly books may be purchased for educational, business, or sales promotional use. Online editions are also available for most titles (*http://my.safari booksonline.com*). For more information, contact our corporate/institutional sales department: (800) 998-9938 or *corporate@oreilly.com*.

Editor: Mike Loukides
Production Editor: Loranah Dimant
Proofreader: Loranah Dimant
Indexer: Fred Brown
Cover Designer: Karen Montgomery
Interior Designer: David Futato

Printing History:
        May 2010:   First Edition.

ISBN: 978-1-449-38788-4

[LSI]   [2012-06-29]

1339848159

Contents

The Bash Shell

This pocket reference covers Bash, particularly version 4.1, the primary shell for GNU/Linux and Mac OS X. Bash is available for Solaris and the various BSD systems, and can be easily compiled for just about any other Unix system. The following topics are covered:

- History
- Overview of features
- Invoking the shell
- Syntax
- Functions
- Variables
- Arithmetic expressions
- Command history
- Programmable completion
- Job control
- Shell options
- Command execution
- Coprocesses
- Restricted shells
- Built-in commands
- Resources

Conventions

Filenames, command names, options and inline examples are shown in `constant width`. Input that a user should type in exactly as-is is shown in **`constant width userinput`**. Items which should be replaced with real data in examples and syntax descriptions are shown in *`constant width replaceable`*. New terms and emphasized items are shown in *italics*. Finally, references of the form *name*(N) refer to the manual page for *name* in section *N* of the online manual (accessed via the `man` command).

History

The original Bourne shell distributed with V7 Unix in 1979 became the standard shell for writing shell scripts. The Bourne shell is still found in `/bin/sh` on many commercial Unix systems. It has not changed that much since its initial release, although it has seen modest enhancements over the years. The most notable new features added were the `CDPATH` variable and a built-in `test` command with System III (circa 1980), command hashing and shell functions for System V Release 2 (circa 1984), and the addition of job control features for System V Release 4 (1989).

Because the Berkeley C shell (`csh`) offered features that were more pleasant for interactive use, such as command history and job control, for a long time the standard practice in the Unix world was to use the Bourne shell for programming and the C shell for daily use. David Korn at Bell Labs was the first developer to enhance the Bourne shell by adding `csh`-like features to it: history, job control, and additional programmability. Eventually, the Korn shell's feature set surpassed both that of the Bourne and C shells, while remaining compatible with the former for shell programming. Today, the POSIX standard defines the "standard shell" language and behavior based on the System V Bourne shell, with a selected subset of features from the Korn shell.

The Free Software Foundation, in keeping with its goal to produce a complete Unix work-alike system, developed a clone of the Bourne shell, written from scratch, named "Bash," the Bourne-Again SHell. Over time, Bash has become a POSIX-compliant version of the shell with many additional features overlapping those of the Korn shell, but Bash is not an exact Korn shell clone. Today, Bash is arguably the most widely used Bourne-derived shell.

Overview of Features

The Bash shell provides the following features:

- Input/output redirection
- Wildcard characters for filename abbreviation
- Shell variables and options for customizing the environment
- A built-in command set for writing shell programs
- Shell functions, for modularizing tasks within a shell program
- Job control
- Command-line editing (using the command syntax of either **vi** or Emacs)
- Access to previous commands (command history)
- Integer arithmetic
- Arrays and arithmetic expressions
- Command-name abbreviation (aliasing)
- Upwards compliance with POSIX
- Internationalization facilities
- An arithmetic **for** loop

Invoking the Shell

The command interpreter for the Bash shell (**bash**) can be invoked as follows:

```
bash  [options]  [arguments]
```

Bash can execute commands from a terminal, from a file (when the first *argument* is a script), or from standard input (if no arguments remain or if **-s** is specified). The shell automatically prints prompts if standard input is a terminal, or if **-i** is given on the command line.

On many systems, **/bin/sh** is a link to Bash. When invoked as **sh**, Bash acts more like the traditional Bourne shell: login shells read **/etc/profile** and **~/.profile**, and regular shells read **$ENV**, if it is set. Full details are available in the *bash*(1) manpage.

Options

-c *str*

    Read commands from string *str*.

-D, --dump-strings

    Print all **$"..."** strings in the program.

-i

    Create an interactive shell (prompt for input).

-l, --login

    Shell is a login shell.

-O *option*

    Enable **shopt** option *option*. Use **+O** to unset *option*.

-p

    Start up as a privileged user. Do not read **$ENV** or **$BASH_ENV**; do not import functions from the environment; and ignore the values of the **BASHOPTS**, **CDPATH**, **GLOBIGNORE**, and **SHELLOPTS** variables. The normal fixed-name startup files (such as **$HOME/.bash_profile**) are read.

-r, --restricted
    Create a restricted shell.

-s

    Read commands from standard input. Output from built-in commands goes to file descriptor 1; all other shell output goes to file descriptor 2.

--debugger
    Read the debugging profile at startup and turn on the **extdebug** option to **shopt**. For use by the Bash debugger (see *http://bashdb.sourceforge.net*).

--dump-po-strings
    Same as -D, but output in GNU **gettext** format.

--help
    Print a usage message and exit successfully.

--init-file *file*, **--rcfile** *file*
    Use *file* as the startup file instead of ~/.bashrc for interactive shells.

--noediting
    Do not use the *readline* library for input, even in an interactive shell.

--noprofile
    Do not read **/etc/profile** or any of the personal startup files.

--norc
    Do not read ~/.bashrc. Enabled automatically when invoked as **sh**.

--posix
    Turn on POSIX mode.

--verbose
    Same as set -v; the shell prints lines as it reads them.

--version
    Print a version message and exit.

-, --

    End option processing.

See the entry for **set** on page 92 for the remaining options.

Arguments

Arguments are assigned in order to the positional parameters **$1**, **$2**, etc. If the first argument is a script, commands are read from it, and the remaining arguments are assigned to **$1**, **$2**, etc. The name of the script is available as **$0**. The script file itself need not be executable, but it must be readable.

Syntax

This section describes the many symbols peculiar to the shell. The topics are arranged as follows:

- Special files
- Filename metacharacters
- Brace expansion
- Quoting
- Command forms
- Redirection forms

Special Files

The shell reads one or more startup files. Some of the files are read only when a shell is a login shell. Bash reads these files:

1. **/etc/profile**. Executed automatically at login.
2. The first file found from this list: **~/.bash_profile**, **~/.bash_login**, or **~/.profile**. Executed automatically at login.
3. **~/.bashrc** is read by every nonlogin shell. However, if invoked as **sh**, Bash instead reads **$ENV**, for POSIX compatibility.

The getpwnam() and getpwuid() functions are the sources of home directories for *~name* abbreviations. (On personal systems, the user database is stored in **/etc/passwd**. However, on networked systems, this information may come from NIS, NIS+, or LDAP, not your workstation password file.)

Filename Metacharacters

*	Match any string of zero or more characters.
?	Match any single character.
[*abc*...]	Match any one of the enclosed characters; a hyphen can specify a range (e.g., a-z, A-Z, 0-9).
[!*abc*...]	Match any character *not* enclosed as above.
~	Home directory of the current user.
~*name*	Home directory of user *name*.
~+	Current working directory (**$PWD**).
~-	Previous working directory (**$OLDPWD**).

With the **extglob** option on:

?(*pattern*)	Match zero or one instance of *pattern*.
*(*pattern*)	Match zero or more instances of *pattern*.
+(*pattern*)	Match one or more instances of *pattern*.
@(*pattern*)	Match exactly one instance of *pattern*.
!(*pattern*)	Match any strings that don't match *pattern*.

This *pattern* can be a sequence of patterns separated by |, meaning that the match applies to any of the patterns. This extended syntax resembles that available in **egrep** and **awk**.

With the **globstar** option on:

**	Match all files and zero or more subdirectories. When followed by a slash, only directories and subdirectories are matched.

Bash supports the POSIX [[=c=]] notation for matching characters that have the same weight, and [[.c.]] for specifying collating sequences. In addition, character classes, of the form [[:class:]], allow you to match the following classes of characters.

Class	Characters matched	Class	Characters matched
alnum	Alphanumeric characters	print	Printable characters
alpha	Alphabetic characters	punct	Punctuation characters
blank	Space or Tab	space	Whitespace characters
cntrl	Control characters	upper	Uppercase characters
digit	Decimal digits	word	[[:word:]] is the same as [[:alnum:]_] (not in POSIX)
graph	Nonspace characters	xdigit	Hexadecimal digits
lower	Lowercase characters		

Examples

```
$ ls new*                  List new and new.1
$ cat ch?                  Match ch9 but not ch10
$ vi [D-R]*                Match files beginning with D through R
$ pr !(*.o|core) | lp      Print files non-object and non-core files
```

CAUTION

On modern systems, ranges such as [D-R] are not portable; the system's locale may include more than just the uppercase letters from D to R in the range.

Brace Expansion

Bash has long supported brace expansion, based on a similar feature from the C shell. Unlike filename metacharacters, brace

---

expansion is purely textual; the words created by brace expansion do not have to match existing files. There are two forms:

pre{X,Y[,Z...]}post
> Expands to `preXpost`, `preYpost`, and so on.

pre{start..end[..incr]}post
> Here, *start*, *end*, and *incr* are all integers. The shell expands them to the full range between *start* and *end*, increasing by *incr* if supplied. Bash ignores leading zeros on *incr*, always treating it as a decimal value.

The prefix and postfix texts are not required for either form. For numeric expansion, *start* or *end* or both may be prefixed with one or more leading zeros. The results of expansion are padded with zeros to the maximum of the widths of *start* and *end*. The value of *incr* is treated as a plain integer, as returned by the C library *strtol*(3) routine. (Thus a leading zero on *incr* causes it to be treated as an octal value.)

Brace expansions may be nested, and the results are *not* sorted. Brace expansion is performed before other expansions, and the opening and closing braces must not be quoted for Bash to recognize them. To avoid conflict with parameter expansion, ${ cannot start a brace expansion.

Examples

```
# Expand textually; no sorting
$ echo hi{DDD,BBB,CCC,AAA}there
hiDDDthere hiBBBthere hiCCCthere hiAAAthere

# Expand, then match ch1, ch2, app1, app2
$ ls {ch,app}?

# Expands to mv info info.old
$ mv info{,.old}

# Simple numeric expansion
$ echo 1 to 10 is {1..10}
1 to 10 is 1 2 3 4 5 6 7 8 9 10
```

```
# Numeric expansion with increment
$ echo 1 to 10 by 2 is {1..10..2}
1 to 10 by 2 is 1 3 5 7 9

# Numeric expansion with zero padding
$ echo 1 to 10 with zeros is {01..10}
1 to 10 with zeros is 01 02 03 04 05 06 07 08 09 10
```

Quoting

Quoting disables a character's special meaning and allows it to be used literally. The following table displays characters that have special meaning.

Character	Meaning
;	Command separator.
&	Background execution.
( )	Command grouping.
|	Pipe.
< > &	Redirection symbols.
* ? [ ] ~ + - @ !	Filename metacharacters.
" ' \	Used in quoting other characters.
`	Command substitution.
$	Variable substitution (or command or arithmetic substitution).
#	Start a comment that continues to the end of the line.
space tab newline	Word separators.

These characters can be used for quoting:

" "

Everything between " and " is taken literally, except for the following characters that keep their special meaning:

$

    Variable (or command and arithmetic) substitution will occur.

`

    Command substitution will occur.

"

    This marks the end of the double quoted string.

' '

Everything between ' and ' is taken literally, except for another '. You cannot embed another ' within such a quoted string.

\

The character following a \ is taken literally. Use within " " to escape ", $, and `. Often used to escape itself, spaces, or newlines.

$" "

Just like " ", except that locale translation is done.

$' '

Similar to ' ', but the quoted text is processed for the following escape sequences.

Sequence	Value	Sequence	Value
\a	Alert	\t	Tab
\b	Backspace	\v	Vertical tab
\cX	Control character X	\nnn	Octal value nnn
\e	Escape	\xnn	Hexadecimal value nn
\E	Escape	\'	Single quote
\f	Form feed	\"	Double quote
\n	Newline	\\	Backslash
\r	Carriage return		

Examples

```
$ echo 'Single quotes "protect" double quotes'
Single quotes "protect" double quotes
$ echo "Well, isn't that \"special\"?"
Well, isn't that "special"?
$ echo "You have `ls | wc -l` files in `pwd`"
You have       43 files in /home/bob
$ echo "The value of \$x is $x"
The value of $x is 100
```

Command Forms

cmd &	Execute *cmd* in background.
cmd1 ; *cmd2*	Command sequence; execute multiple *cmd*s on the same line.
{ *cmd1* ; *cmd2* ; }	Execute commands as a group in the current shell.
(*cmd1* ; *cmd2*)	Execute commands as a group in a subshell.
cmd1 | *cmd2*	Pipe; use output from *cmd1* as input to *cmd2*.
cmd1 `cmd2`	Command substitution; use *cmd2* output as arguments to *cmd1*.
cmd1 $(*cmd2*)	POSIX shell command substitution; nesting is allowed.
cmd $((*expression*))	POSIX shell arithmetic substitution. Use the result of *expression* as argument to *cmd*.
cmd1 && *cmd2*	AND; execute *cmd1* and then (if *cmd1* succeeds) *cmd2*. This is a "short circuit" operation: *cmd2* is never executed if *cmd1* fails.
cmd1 || *cmd2*	OR; execute either *cmd1* or (if *cmd1* fails) *cmd2*. This is a "short circuit" operation; *cmd2* is never executed if *cmd1* succeeds.
! *cmd*	NOT; execute *cmd*, and produce a zero exit status if *cmd* exits with a nonzero status. Otherwise, produce a nonzero status when *cmd* exits with a zero status.

Examples

```
# Format in the background
$ nroff file > file.txt &

# Execute sequentially
$ cd; ls

# All output is redirected
$ (date; who; pwd) > logfile

# Sort file, page output, then print
$ sort file | pr -3 | lp

# Edit files found by grep
$ vi `grep -l ifdef *.cpp`

# Specify a list of files to search
$ egrep '(yes|no)' `cat list`

# POSIX version of previous
$ egrep '(yes|no)' $(cat list)

# Faster; not in POSIX
$ egrep '(yes|no)' $(< list)

# Print file if it contains the pattern
$ grep XX file && lp file

# Otherwise, echo an error message
$ grep XX file || echo "XX not found"
```

Redirection Forms

File descriptor	Name	Common abbreviation	Typical default
0	Standard input	stdin	Keyboard
1	Standard output	stdout	Screen
2	Standard error	stderr	Screen

The usual input source or output destination can be changed, as seen in the following sections.

Simple redirection

cmd > *file*
> Send output of *cmd* to *file* (overwrite).

cmd >> *file*
> Send output of *cmd* to *file* (append).

cmd < *file*
> Take input for *cmd* from *file*.

cmd << *text*
> The contents of the shell script up to a line identical to *text* become the standard input for *cmd* (*text* can be stored in a shell variable). This command form is sometimes called a *here document*. Input is typed at the keyboard or in the shell program. Commands that typically use this syntax include **cat**, **ex**, and **sed**. (If <<- is used, leading tabs are stripped from the contents of the here document, and the tabs are ignored when comparing input with the end-of-input *text* marker.) If any part of *text* is quoted, the input is passed through verbatim. Otherwise, the contents are processed for variable, command, and arithmetic substitutions.

cmd <<< *word*
> Supply text of *word*, with trailing newline, as input to *cmd*. (This is known as a *here string*, from the free version of the **rc** shell.)

cmd <> *file*
> Open *file* for reading *and* writing on the standard input. The contents are not destroyed.[*]

cmd >| *file*
> Send output of *cmd* to *file* (overwrite), even if the shell's **noclobber** option is set.

---

[*] With <, the file is opened read-only, and writes on the file descriptor will fail. With <>, the file is opened read-write; it is up to the application to actually take advantage of this.

Redirection using file descriptors

cmd >&n

    Send *cmd* output to file descriptor *n*.

cmd m>&n

    Same as previous, except that output that would normally go to file descriptor *m* is sent to file descriptor *n* instead.

cmd >&-

    Close standard output.

cmd <&n

    Take input for *cmd* from file descriptor *n*.

cmd m<&n

    Same as previous, except that input that would normally come from file descriptor *m* comes from file descriptor *n* instead.

cmd <&-

    Close standard input.

cmd <&n-

    Move file descriptor *n* to standard input by duplicating it and then closing the original.

cmd >&n-

    Move file descriptor *n* to standard output by duplicating it and then closing the original.

Multiple redirection

cmd 2>file

    Send standard error to *file*; standard output remains the same (e.g., the screen).

cmd > file 2>&1

    Send both standard output and standard error to *file*.

cmd >& file

    Same as previous.

cmd &> file

    Same as previous. Preferred form.

cmd &>> *file*
> Append both standard output and standard error to *file*.

cmd > *f1* 2> *f2*
> Send standard output to file *f1* and standard error to file *f2*.

cmd | tee *files*
> Send output of *cmd* to standard output (usually the terminal) and to *files*. See *tee*(1).

cmd 2>&1 | tee *files*
> Send standard output and error output of *cmd* through a pipe to tee to standard output (usually the terminal) and to *files*.

cmd |& tee *files*
> Same as previous.

Bash allows multidigit file descriptor numbers without any special syntax. Most other shells either require a special syntax or do not offer the feature at all.

Bash also allows {*variablename*} instead of a file descriptor number in redirections. In such a case, the shell uses a file descriptor number greater than nine, and assigns the value to the named shell variable.

NOTE

No space is allowed between file descriptors and a redirection symbol; spacing is optional in the other cases.

Process substitution

cmd <(*command*)
> Run *command* with its output connected to a named pipe or an open file in /dev/fd, and place the file's name in the argument list of *cmd*.

cmd >(*command*)
> Run *command* with its input connected to a named pipe or an open file in /dev/fd, and place the file's name in the argument list of *cmd*.

Process substitution is available on systems that support either named pipes (FIFOs) or accessing open files via filenames in /dev/fd. (This is true of all modern Unix systems.) It provides a way to create non-linear pipelines.

Special filenames

Bash recognizes several special filenames in redirections and interprets them internally, even if you have such a file on your system:

/dev/stdin
> A duplicate of file descriptor zero.

/dev/stdout
> A duplicate of file descriptor one.

/dev/stderr
> A duplicate of file descriptor two.

/dev/fd/*n*
> A duplicate of file descriptor *n*.

/dev/tcp/*host*/*port*
> Bash opens a TCP connection to *host*, which is either a hostname or IP address, on port *port* and uses the file descriptor in the redirection.

/dev/udp/*host*/*port*
> Bash opens a UDP connection to *host*, which is either a hostname or IP address, on port *port* and uses the file descriptor in the redirection.

Examples

```
$ cat part1 > book            Copy part1 to book
$ cat part2 part3 >> book      Append part2 and part3k
$ mail tim < report           Send report to the big boss
$ sed 's/^/XX /g' << END_ARCHIVE   Here document is sed's input
> This is often how a shell archive is "wrapped",
> bundling text for distribution.  You would normally
> run sed from a shell program, not from the command line.
> END_ARCHIVE
XX This is often how a shell archive is "wrapped",
XX bundling text for distribution.  You would normally
XX run sed from a shell program, not from the command line.
```

To redirect standard output to standard error:

```
$ echo "Usage error: see administrator" 1>&2
```

The following command sends output (files found) to filelist, and error messages (inaccessible files) to no_access:

```
$ find / -print > filelist 2>no_access
```

The following demonstrates how Bash assigns file descriptor numbers to named variables:

```
$ echo foo {foofd}> /tmp/xyzzy          Save file descriptor number
foo
$ echo $foofd
11
```

The following sorts two files and presents the differences between the results using the diff command:

```
$ diff <(sort file1) <(sort file2)
```

Functions

A shell *function* is a grouping of commands within a shell script. Shell functions let you modularize your program by dividing it up into separate tasks. This way, the code for each task is not repeated every time you need to perform the task. The POSIX shell syntax for defining a function follows the Bourne shell:

```
name () {
    function body's code comes here
} [redirections]
```

Functions are invoked just as are regular shell built-in commands or external commands. The command-line parameters $1, $2, and so on receive the function's arguments, temporarily hiding the global values of $1, etc. For example:

```
# fatal --- print an error message and die:

fatal () {
    # Messages go to standard error.
    echo "$0: fatal error:" "$@" >&2
    exit 1
}
```

```
...
if [ $# = 0 ]    # not enough arguments
then
    fatal not enough arguments
fi
```

A function may use the **return** command to return an exit value to the calling shell program. Be careful *not* to use **exit** from within a function unless you really wish to terminate the entire program.

Per the POSIX standard, any *redirections* given with the function definition are evaluated when the function executes, not when it is defined.

Bash allows you to define functions using a slightly different syntax, as follows:

```
function name [()] { body } [redirections]
```

When using the **function** keyword, the parentheses following the function name are optional.

Functions share traps with the "parent" shell as described in the following table.

Trap type	Shared/not shared
Signal-based traps	Shared until the function redefines the trap
DEBUG	Not shared unless function tracing is enabled (set -T or set -o functrace)
ERR	Not shared unless error tracing is enabled (set -E or set -o errtrace)
EXIT	Shared until the function redefines the trap
RETURN	Not shared unless function tracing is enabled (set -T or set -o functrace)

Functions may have local variables, and they may be recursive. Unlike the Korn shell, the syntax used to define a function is irrelevant.

Function names do not have to be valid shell identifiers (just as external commands do not have to have names that are valid shell identifiers).

Variables

This section describes the following:

- Variable assignment
- Variable substitution
- Built-in shell variables
- Other shell variables
- Arrays
- Special prompt strings

Variable Assignment

Variable names consist of any number of letters, digits, or underscores. Upper- and lowercase letters are distinct, and names may not start with a digit. Variables are assigned values using the = operator. There may *not* be any whitespace between the variable name and the value. You can make multiple assignments on the same line by separating each one with whitespace:

```
firstname=Arnold lastname=Robbins numkids=4 numpets=1
```

By convention, names for variables used or set by the shell have all uppercase letters; however, you can use uppercase names in your scripts if you use a name that isn't special to the shell.

By default, the shell treats variable values as strings, even if the value of the string is all digits. However, when a value is assigned to an integer variable (created via `declare -i`), Bash evaluates the righthand side of the assignment as an expression (see the section "Arithmetic Expressions" on page 36). For example:

```
$ i=5+3 ; echo $i
5+3
$ declare -i jj ; jj=5+3 ;  echo $jj
8
```

The += operator allows you to add or append the righthand side of the assignment to an existing value. Integer variables treat the righthand side as an expression, which is evaluated and added to the value. Arrays add the new elements to the array (see the section "Arrays" on page 33). For example:

```
$ name=Arnold
$ name+=" Robbins" ; echo $name          String variable
Arnold Robbins
$ declare -i jj ; jj=3+5 ; echo $jj       Integer variable
8
$ jj+=2+4 ; echo $jj
14
$ pets=(blacky rusty)                     Array variable
$ echo ${pets[*]}
blacky rusty
$ pets+=(raincloud sophie)
$ echo ${pets[*]}
blacky rusty raincloud sophie
```

Variable Substitution

No spaces should be used in the following expressions. The colon (:) is optional; if it's included, *var* must be nonnull as well as set.

var=value ...	Set each variable *var* to a *value*.
${*var*}	Use value of *var*; braces are optional if *var* is separated from the following text. They are required for array variables.
${*var*:-*value*}	Use *var* if set; otherwise, use *value*.
${*var*:=*value*}	Use *var* if set; otherwise, use *value* and assign *value* to *var*.
${*var*:?*value*}	Use *var* if set; otherwise, print *value* and exit (if not interactive). If *value* isn't supplied, print the phrase parameter null or not set.
${*var*:+*value*}	Use *value* if *var* is set; otherwise, use nothing.

`${#var}`	Use the length of *var*.
`${#*}`	Use the number of positional parameters.
`${#@}`	Same as previous.
`${var#pattern}`	Use value of *var* after removing text matching *pattern* from the left. Remove the shortest matching piece.
`${var##pattern}`	Same as *#pattern*, but remove the longest matching piece.
`${var%pattern}`	Use value of *var* after removing text matching *pattern* from the right. Remove the shortest matching piece.
`${var%%pattern}`	Same as *%pattern*, but remove the longest matching piece.
`${var^pattern}`	Convert the case of *var* to uppercase. The *pattern* is evaluated as for filename matching. If the first letter of *var* matches the pattern, it is converted to uppercase. *var* can be * or @, in which case the positional parameters are modified. *var* can also be an array subscripted by * or @, in which case the substitution is applied to all the elements of the array.
`${var^^pattern}`	Same as *^pattern*, but apply the match to every letter in the string.
`${var,pattern}`	Same as *^pattern*, but convert matching characters to lower case. Applies only to the first character in the string.
`${var,,pattern}`	Same as *,pattern*, but apply the match to every letter in the string.
`${!prefix*}`, `${!prefix@}`	List of variables whose names begin with *prefix*.
`${var:pos}`, `${var:pos:len}`	Starting at position *pos* (0-based) in variable *var*, extract *len* characters, or extract rest of string if no *len*. *pos* and *len* may be arithmetic expressions.
	When *var* is * or @, the expansion is performed upon the positional parameters. If *pos* is zero, then $0 is included in the resulting list. Similarly, *var* can be an array indexed by * or @.

`${var/pat/repl}`	Use value of *var*, with first match of *pat* replaced with *repl*.
`${var/pat}`	Use value of *var*, with first match of *pat* deleted.
`${var//pat/repl}`	Use value of *var*, with every match of *pat* replaced with *repl*.
`${var/#pat/repl}`	Use value of *var*, with match of *pat* replaced with *repl*. Match must occur at beginning of the value.
`${var/%pat/repl}`	Use value of *var*, with match of *pat* replaced with *repl*. Match must occur at end of the value.
`${!var}`	Use value of *var* as name of variable whose value should be used (indirect reference).

Bash provides a special syntax that lets one variable indirectly reference another:

```
$ greet="hello, world"        Create initial variable
$ friendly_message=greet      Aliasing variable
$ echo ${!friendly_message}   Use the alias
hello, world
```

Examples

```
$ u=up d=down blank=          Assign values to 3 variables
        (last is null)
$ echo ${u}root               Braces are needed here
uproot
$ echo ${u-$d}                Display value of u or d; u is set,
        so print it
up
$ echo ${tmp-`date`}          If tmp not set, execute date
Mon Apr 12 14:33:16 EDT 2010
$ echo ${blank="no data"}     blank is set, so it is printed (blank line)
$ echo ${blank:="no data"}    blank is set but null, print string
no data
$ echo $blank                 blank now has a new value
no data

# Take the current directory name and remove the longest
# character string ending with /, which removes the
# leading pathname and leaves the tail
$ tail=${PWD##*/}
```

```
# Use a famous word
$ word=supercalifragilisticexpialidocious

# Modify the case of the first character
$ echo ${word^[r-t]}
Supercalifragilisticexpialidocious

# Modify the case of all matching characters
$ echo ${word^^[r-t]}
SupeRcalifRagiliSTicexpialidociouS
```

Built-in Shell Variables

Built-in variables are automatically set by the shell and are typically used inside shell scripts. Built-in variables can make use of the variable substitution patterns shown previously. Note that the $ is not actually part of the variable name, although the variable is always referenced this way. The following are available in any Bourne-compatible shell:

$#   Number of command-line arguments.

$-   Options currently in effect (supplied on command line or to set). The shell sets some options automatically.

$?   Exit value of last executed command.

$$ Process number of the shell.

$!   Process number of last background command.

$0   First word; that is, the command name. This will have the full pathname if it was found via a PATH search.

$n   Individual arguments on command line (positional parameters). The Bourne shell allows only nine parameters to be referenced directly (n = 1–9); Bash allows n to be greater than 9 if specified as ${n}.

$*, $@ All arguments on command line ($1 $2 ...).

"$*"   All arguments on command line as one string ("$1 $2…"). The values are separated by the first character in $IFS.

"$@"   All arguments on command line, individually quoted ("$1" "$2" ...).

Bash automatically sets the following additional variables:

`$_`	Temporary variable; initialized to path-name of script or program being executed. Later, stores the last argument of previous command. Also stores name of matching **MAIL** file during mail checks.
`BASH`	The full pathname used to invoke this instance of Bash.
`BASHOPTS`	A read-only, colon-separated list of shell options that are currently enabled. Each item in the list is a valid option for **shopt -s**. If this variable exists in the environment when Bash starts up, it sets the indicated options before executing any startup files.
`BASHPID`	The process ID of the current Bash process. In some cases, this can differ from **$$**.
`BASH_ALIASES`	Associative array variable. Each element holds an alias defined with the **alias** command. Adding an element to this array creates a new alias; removing an element removes the corresponding alias.
`BASH_ARGC`	Array variable. Each element holds the number of arguments for the corresponding function or dot-script invocation. Set only in extended debug mode, with **shopt -s extdebug**. Cannot be unset.
`BASH_ARGV`	An array variable similar to **BASH_ARGC**. Each element is one of the arguments passed to a function or dot-script. It functions as a stack, with values being pushed on at each call. Thus, the last element is the last argument to the most recent function or script invocation. Set only in extended debug mode, with **shopt -s extdebug**. Cannot be unset.
`BASH_CMDS`	Associative array variable. Each element refers to a command in the internal hash table maintained by the **hash** command. The index is the command name and the value is the full path to the command. Adding an

	element to this array adds a command to the hash table; removing an element removes the corresponding entry.
BASH_COMMAND	The command currently executing or about to be executed. Inside a trap handler, it is the command running when the trap was invoked.
BASH_EXECUTION_STRING	The string argument passed to the -c option.
BASH_LINENO	Array variable, corresponding to BASH_SOURCE and FUNCNAME. For any given function number i (starting at zero), ${FUNCNAME[i]} was invoked in file ${BASH_SOURCE[i]} on line ${BASH_LINENO[i]}. The information is stored with the most recent function invocation first. Cannot be unset.
BASH_REMATCH	Array variable, assigned by the =~ operator of the [[ ]] construct. Index zero is the text that matched the entire pattern. The other indices are the text matched by parenthesized subexpressions. This variable is read-only.
BASH_SOURCE	Array variable, containing source filenames. Each element corresponds to those in FUNCNAME and BASH_LINENO. Cannot be unset.
BASH_SUBSHELL	This variable is incremented by one each time a subshell or subshell environment is created.
BASH_VERSINFO[0]	The major version number, or release, of Bash.
BASH_VERSINFO[1]	The minor version number, or version, of Bash.
BASH_VERSINFO[2]	The patch level.
BASH_VERSINFO[3]	The build version.
BASH_VERSINFO[4]	The release status.
BASH_VERSINFO[5]	The machine type; same value as in $MACHTYPE.

BASH_VERSION	A string describing the version of Bash.
COMP_CWORD	For programmable completion. Index into COMP_WORDS, indicating the current cursor position.
COMP_KEY	For programmable completion. The key, or final key in a sequence, that caused the invocation of the current completion function.
COMP_LINE	For programmable completion. The current command line.
COMP_POINT	For programmable completion. The position of the cursor as a character index in $COMP_LINE.
COMP_TYPE	For programmable completion. A character describing the type of programmable completion. The character is one of Tab for normal completion, ? for a completions list after two Tabs, ! for the list of alternatives on partial word completion, @ for completions if the word is modified, or % for menu completion.
COMP_WORDBREAKS	For programmable completion. The characters that the *readline* library treats as word separators when doing word completion.
COMP_WORDS	For programmable completion. Array variable containing the individual words on the command line.
COPROC	Array variable that holds the file descriptors used for communicating with an unnamed coprocess. For more information, see "Coprocesses" on page 53.
DIRSTACK	Array variable, containing the contents of the directory stack as displayed by **dirs**. Changing existing elements modifies the stack, but only **pushd** and **popd** can add or remove elements from the stack.
EUID	Read-only variable with the numeric effective UID of the current user.

FUNCNAME	Array variable, containing function names. Each element corresponds to those in BASH_SOURCE and BASH_LINENO.
GROUPS	Array variable, containing the list of numeric group IDs in which the current user is a member.
HISTCMD	The history number of the current command.
HOSTNAME	The name of the current host.
HOSTTYPE	A string that describes the host system.
LINENO	Current line number within the script or function.
MACHTYPE	A string that describes the host system in the GNU *cpu-company-system* format.
MAPFILE	Default array for the mapfile and readarray commands. See the entry for mapfile on page 86 for more information.
OLDPWD	Previous working directory (set by cd).
OPTARG	Value of argument to last option processed by getopts.
OPTIND	Numerical index of OPTARG.
OSTYPE	A string that describes the operating system.
PIPESTATUS	Array variable, containing the exit statuses of the commands in the most recent foreground pipeline.
PPID	Process number of this shell's parent.
PWD	Current working directory (set by cd).
RANDOM[=*n*]	Generate a new random number with each reference; start with integer *n*, if given.
READLINE_LINE	For use with bind -x. The contents of the editing buffer are available in this variable.
READLINE_POINT	For use with bind -x. The index in $READLINE_LINE of the insertion point.
REPLY	Default reply; used by select and read.

SECONDS[=*n*]	Number of seconds since the shell was started, or, if *n* is given, number of seconds since the assignment + *n*.
SHELLOPTS	A read-only, colon-separated list of shell options (for set -o). If set in the environment at startup, Bash enables each option present in the list before reading any startup files.
SHLVL	Incremented by one every time a new Bash starts up.
UID	Read-only variable with the numeric real UID of the current user.

Many of these variables provide support for either the Bash Debugger (see *http://bashdb.sourceforge.net*) or for programmable completion (see the section "Programmable Completion" on page 41).

Other Shell Variables

The following variables are not automatically set by the shell, although many of them can influence the shell's behavior. You typically use them in your .bash_profile or .profile file, where you can define them to suit your needs. Variables can be assigned values by issuing commands of the form:

```
variable=value
```

This list includes the type of value expected when defining these variables:

BASH_ENV	If set at startup, names a file to be processed for initialization commands. The value undergoes parameter expansion, command substitution, and arithmetic expansion before being interpreted as a filename.
BASH_XTRACEFD=*n*	File descriptor to which Bash writes trace output (from set -x).

`CDPATH=`*dirs*	Directories searched by cd; allows short-cuts in changing directories; unset by default.
`COLUMNS=`*n*	Screen's column width; used in line edit modes and select lists.
`COMPREPLY=(`*words* `…)`	Array variable from which Bash reads the possible completions generated by a completion function.
`EMACS`	If the value starts with t, Bash assumes it's running in an Emacs buffer and disables line editing.
`ENV=`*file*	Name of script that is executed at startup in POSIX mode or when Bash is invoked as `/bin/sh`; useful for storing alias and function definitions. For example, `ENV=`$HOME/.shellrc.
`FCEDIT=`*file*	Editor used by fc command. The default is `/bin/ed` when Bash is in POSIX mode. Otherwise, the default is $EDITOR if set, vi if unset.
`FIGNORE=`*patlist*	Colon-separated list of patterns describing the set of filenames to ignore when doing filename completion.
`GLOBIGNORE=`*patlist*	Colon-separated list of patterns describing the set of filenames to ignore during pattern matching.
`HISTCONTROL=`*list*	Colon-separated list of values controlling how commands are saved in the history file. Recognized values are ignoredups, ignorespace, ignoreboth, and erasedups.
`HISTFILE=`*file*	File in which to store command history.
`HISTFILESIZE=`*n*	Number of lines to be kept in the history file. This may be different from the number of commands.
`HISTIGNORE=`*list*	A colon-separated list of patterns that must match the entire command line. Matching lines are *not* saved in the history file. An unescaped & in a pattern matches the previous history line.

HISTSIZE=*n*	Number of history commands to be kept in the history file.
HISTTIMEFORMAT=*string*	A format string for *strftime*(3) to use for printing timestamps along with commands from the **history** command. If set (even if null), Bash saves timestamps in the history file along with the commands.
HOME=*dir*	Home directory; set by **login** (from **/etc/passwd** file).
HOSTFILE=*file*	Name of a file in the same format as **/etc/hosts** that Bash should use to find hostnames for hostname completion.
IFS='*chars*'	Input field separators; default is space, Tab, and newline.
IGNOREEOF=*n*	Numeric value indicating how many successive EOF characters must be typed before Bash exits. If null or nonnumeric value, default is 10.
INPUTRC=*file*	Initialization file for the *readline* library. This overrides the default value of **~/.inputrc**.
LANG=*locale*	Default value for locale; used if no LC_* variables are set.
LC_ALL=*locale*	Current locale; overrides **LANG** and the other LC_* variables.
LC_COLLATE=*locale*	Locale to use for character collation (sorting order).
LC_CTYPE=*locale*	Locale to use for character class functions. (See the section "Filename Metacharacters" on page 7.)
LC_MESSAGES=*locale*	Locale to use for translating **$**"..." strings.
LC_NUMERIC=*locale*	Locale to use for the decimal-point character.
LC_TIME=*locale*	Locale to use for date and time formats.
LINES=*n*	Screen's height; used for **select** lists.
MAIL=*file*	Default file to check for incoming mail; set by **login**.

`MAILCHECK=n`	Number of seconds between mail checks; default is 600 (10 minutes).
`MAILPATH=files`	One or more files, delimited by a colon, to check for incoming mail. Along with each file, you may supply an optional message that the shell prints when the file increases in size. Messages are separated from the filename by a ? character, and the default message is `You have mail in $_`. `$_` is replaced with the name of the file. For example, you might have `MAIL PATH="$MAIL?Candygram!:/etc/motd?New Login Message"`
`OPTERR=n`	When set to 1 (the default value), Bash prints error messages from the built-in **getopts** command.
`PATH=dirlist`	One or more pathnames, delimited by colons, in which to search for commands to execute. The default for many systems is `/bin:/usr/bin`. On Solaris, the default is `/usr/bin:`. However, the standard startup scripts change it to `/usr/bin:/usr/ucb:/etc:`.
`POSIXLY_CORRECT=string`	When set at startup or while running, Bash enters POSIX mode, disabling behavior and modifying features that conflict with the POSIX standard.
`PROMPT_COMMAND=command`	If set, Bash executes this command each time before printing the primary prompt.
`PROMPT_DIRTRIM=n`	Indicates how many trailing directory components to retain for the \w or \W special prompt strings (see the section "Special Prompt Strings" on page 35). Elided components are replaced with an ellipsis.
`PS1=string`	Primary prompt string; default is **$**.
`PS2=string`	Secondary prompt (used in multiline commands); default is **>**.
`PS3=string`	Prompt string in **select** loops; default is **#?**.

PS4=*string*	Prompt string for execution trace (bash -x or set -x); default is +.
SHELL=*file*	Name of user's default shell (e.g., /bin/sh). Bash sets this if it's not in the environment at startup.
TERM=*string*	Terminal type.
TIMEFORMAT=*string*	A format string for the output from the time keyword.
TMOUT=*n*	If no command is typed after *n* seconds, exit the shell. Also affects the read command and the select loop.
TMPDIR=*directory*	Place temporary files created and used by the shell in *directory*.
auto_resume=*list*	Enables the use of simple strings for resuming stopped jobs. With a value of exact, the string must match a command name exactly. With a value of substring, it can match a substring of the command name.
histchars=*chars*	Two or three characters that control Bash's csh-style history expansion. The first character signals a history event, the second is the "quick substitution" character, and the third indicates the start of a comment. The default value is !^#. See the section "C-Shell–Style History" on page 39.

Arrays

Bash provides two kinds of arrays: *indexed arrays*, where the indices are integers zero and above, and *associative arrays*, where the indices are strings.

Indexed arrays

Bash supports one-dimensional arrays. The first element is numbered zero. Bash has no limit on the number of elements. Arrays are initialized with a special form of assignment:

```
message=(hi there how are you today)
```

where the specified values become elements of the array. Individual elements may also be assigned to:

```
message[0]=hi                    This is the hard way
message[1]=there
message[2]=how
message[3]=are
message[4]=you
message[5]=today
```

Declaring indexed arrays is not required. Any valid reference to a subscripted variable can create an array.

When referencing arrays, use the ${ ... } syntax. This isn't needed when referencing arrays inside (( )) (the form of **let** that does automatic quoting). Note that [and] are typed literally (i.e., they don't stand for optional syntax).

${*name*[*i*]}	Use element *i* of array *name*. *i* can be any arithmetic expression as described under **let**.
${*name*}	Use element 0 of array *name*.
${*name*[*]}	Use all elements of array *name*.
${*name*[@]}	Same as previous.
${#*name*[*]}	Use the number of elements in array *name*.
${#*name*[@]}	Same as previous.

Associative arrays

Bash provides associative arrays, where the indices are strings instead of numbers (as in **awk**). In this case, [and] act like double quotes. Associative arrays must be declared by using the **-A** option to the **declare**, **local**, and **readonly** commands. A special syntax allows assigning to multiple elements at once:

```
data=([joe]=30 [mary]=25)        Associative array assignment
message=([0]=hi [2]=there)       Indexed array assignment works, too
```

The values would be retrieved as ${data[joe]} and ${data[mary]}.

The special expansions for retrieving all the indices of an associative array work just as they do for indexed arrays.

Special Prompt Strings

Bash processes the values of PS1, PS2, and PS4 for the following special escape sequences:

\a	An ASCII BEL character (octal 07).
\A	The current time in 24-hour HH:MM format.
\d	The date in "weekday month day" format.
\D{format}	The date as specified by the *strftime*(3) format *format*. The braces are required.
\e	An ASCII Escape character (octal 033).
\h	The hostname, up to the first period.
\H	The full hostname.
\j	The current number of jobs.
\l	The basename of the shell's terminal device.
\n	A newline character.
\r	A carriage return character.
\s	The name of the shell (basename of $0).
\t	The current time in 24-hour HH:MM:SS format.
\T	The current time in 12-hour HH:MM:SS format.
\u	The current user's username.
\v	The version of Bash.
\V	The release (version plus patchlevel) of Bash.
\w	The current directory, with $HOME abbreviated as ~. See also the description of the PROMPT_DIRTRIM variable.
\W	The basename of the current directory, with $HOME abbreviated as ~. See also the description of the PROMPT_DIRTRIM variable.
\!	The history number of this command (stored in the history).
\#	The command number of this command (count of commands executed by the current shell).
\$	If the effective UID is 0, a #; otherwise, a $.
\@	The current time in 12-hour a.m./p.m. format.

\\nnn	The character represented by octal value *nnn*.
\\\\	A literal backslash.
\\[	Start a sequence of nonprinting characters, such as for highlighting or changing colors on a terminal.
\\]	End a sequence of nonprinting characters.

The PS1, PS2, and PS4 variables undergo substitution for escape sequences, variable substitution, command substitution, and arithmetic substitution. The escape sequences are processed first, and then, if the **promptvars** shell option is enabled via the **shopt** command (the default), the substitutions are performed.

Arithmetic Expressions

The **let** command performs arithmetic. Bash is restricted to integer arithmetic. The shell provides a way to substitute arithmetic values (for use as command arguments or in variables); base conversion is also possible:

$((*expr*))	Use the value of the enclosed arithmetic expression.
B#*n*	Interpret integer *n* in numeric base *B*. For example, 8#100 specifies the octal equivalent of decimal 64.

Operators

The shell uses arithmetic operators from the C programming language, in decreasing order of precedence.

Operator	Description
++ --	Auto-increment and auto-decrement, both prefix and postfix
+ -	Unary plus and minus
! ~	Logical negation and binary inversion (one's complement)
**	Exponentiation[a]
* / %	Multiplication, division, modulus (remainder)

Operator	Description
+ -	Addition, subtraction
<< >>	Bitwise left shift, bitwise right shift
< <= > >=	Less than, less than or equal to, greater than, greater than or equal to
== !=	Equality, inequality (both evaluated left to right)
&	Bitwise AND
^	Bitwise exclusive OR
|	Bitwise OR
&&	Logical AND (short circuit)
||	Logical OR (short circuit)
?:	Inline conditional evaluation
= += -=	
*= /= %=	
<<= >>=	Assignment
&= ^= |=	
,	Sequential expression evaluation

a The ** operator is right-associative. Prior to version 3.1, it was left-associative.

Examples

```
let "count=0" "i = i + 1"        Assign values to i and count
let "num % 2"                     Exit successfully if num is even
(( percent >= 0 && \
   percent <= 100 ))              Test the range of a value
```

See the entry for `let` on page 85 for more information and examples.

Command History

The shell lets you display or modify previous commands. Using the `history` command, you can manage the list of commands kept in the shell's history; see `history` on page 81 for more information. This section focuses on the facilities for editing stored commands. Commands in the history list can be modified using:

- Line-edit mode
- The `fc` command
- C-shell–style history

Line-Edit Mode

Line-edit mode emulates many features of the **vi** and Emacs editors. The history list is treated like a file. When the editor is invoked, you type editing keystrokes to move to the command line you want to execute. You can also change the line before executing it. When you're ready to issue the command, press the Enter key.

Emacs editing mode is the default. To control command-line editing, you must use either `set -o vi` or `set -o emacs`; Bash does not use variables to specify the editor.

Note that the **vi** editing mode starts in input mode; to type a **vi** command, press the Escape key first.

Common editing keystrokes

vi	Emacs	Result
k	CTRL-p	Get previous command.
j	CTRL-n	Get next command.
/string	CTRL-r string	Get previous command containing *string*.
h	CTRL-b	Move back one character.
l	CTRL-f	Move forward one character.
b	ESC-b	Move back one word.
w	ESC-f	Move forward one word.
X	DEL	Delete previous character.
x	CTRL-d	Delete character under cursor.
dw	ESC-d	Delete word forward.

vi	Emacs	Result
db	ESC-h	Delete word backward.
xp	CTRL-t	Transpose two characters.

Both editing modes allow you to use the cursor keys to move around within the saved history.

The fc Command

fc stands for either "find command" or "fix command," because it does both jobs. Use fc -l to list history commands and fc -e to edit them. See the entry for fc on page 76 for more information.

Examples

`$ history`	*List the last 16 commands*
`$ fc -l 20 30`	*List commands 20 through 30*
`$ fc -l -5`	*List the last 5 commands*
`$ fc -l cat`	*List all commands since the last cat command*
`$ fc -l 50`	*List all commands since command 50*
`$ fc -ln 5 > doit`	*Save command 5 to file doit*
`$ fc -e vi 5 20`	*Edit commands 5 through 20 using vi*
`$ fc -e emacs`	*Edit previous command using emacs*

Interactive line-editing is easier to use than fc, because you can move up and down in the saved command history using your favorite editor commands (as long as your favorite editor is either vi or Emacs!). You may also use the Up and Down arrow keys to traverse the command history.

C-Shell–Style History

Besides the interactive editing features and POSIX fc command, Bash supports a command-line editing mode similar to that of the Berkeley C shell (csh). It can be disabled using set +H. Many users prefer the interactive editing features, but for those whose "finger habits" are still those of csh, this feature comes in handy.

Event designators

Event designators mark a command-line word as a history substitution.

Command	Description
!	Begin a history substitution.
!!	Previous command.
!*n*	Command number *n* in history list.
!-*n*	*n* th command back from current command.
!*string*	Most recent command that starts with *string*.
!?*string*[?]	Most recent command that contains *string*.
#	Current command line up to this point (fairly useless).
^*old*^*new*^	Quick substitution; change string *old* to *new* in previous command, and execute modified command.

Word substitution

Word specifiers allow you to retrieve individual words from previous command lines. They follow an initial event specifier, separated by a colon. The colon is optional if followed by any of the following: ^, $, *, -, or %.

Specifier	Description
:0	Command name
:*n*	Argument number *n*
^	First argument
$	Last argument
%	Argument matched by a !?*string*? search
:*n-m*	Arguments *n* through *m*
-*m*	Words 0 through *m*; same as :0-*m*
:*n-*	Arguments *n* through next-to-last
:*n**	Arguments *n* through last; same as *n*-$
*	All arguments; same as ^-$ or 1-$

History modifiers

There are several ways to modify command and word substitutions. The printing, substitution, and quoting modifiers are shown in the following table.

Modifier	Description
:p	Display command, but don't execute.
:s/*old*/*new*	Substitute string *new* for *old*, first instance only.
:gs/*old*/*new*	Substitute string *new* for *old*, all instances.
:as/*old*/*new*	Same as :gs.
:Gs/*old*/*new*	Like :gs, but apply the substitution to all the words in the command line.
:&	Repeat previous substitution (:s or ^ command), first instance only.
:g&	Repeat previous substitution, all instances.
:q	Quote a word list.
:x	Quote separate words.

The truncation modifiers are shown in the following table.

Modifier	Description
:r	Extract the first available pathname root (the portion before the last period).
:e	Extract the first available pathname extension (the portion after the last period).
:h	Extract the first available pathname header (the portion before the last slash).
:t	Extract the first available pathname tail (the portion after the last slash).

Programmable Completion

Bash and the *readline* library provide *completion* facilities, whereby you can type part of a command name, hit the Tab key, and Bash will fill in part or all of the rest of the command or filename. *Programmable completion* lets you, as a shell programmer, write code to customize the list of possible completions that Bash will present for a particular partially entered word. This is accomplished through the combination of several facilities:

- The `complete` command allows you to provide a completion specification, or *compspec*, for individual commands. You specify, via various options, how to tailor the list of possible completions for the particular command. This is simple, but adequate for many needs. (See the entry for `complete` on page 63.)

- For more flexibility, you can use `complete -F` *funcname command*. This tells Bash to call *funcname* to provide the list of completions for *command*. You write the *funcname* function.

- Within the code for a `-F` function, the COMP* shell variables provide information about the current command line. `COMPREPLY` is an array into which the function places the final list of completion results.

- Also within the code for a `-F` function, you may use the `compgen` command to generate a list of results, such as "usernames that begin with **a**" or "all set variables." The intent is that such results would be used with an array assignment:

```
...
COMPREPLY=( $( compgen options arguments ) )
...
```

Compspecs may be associated with either a full pathname for a command or, more commonly, an unadorned command name (`/usr/bin/man` versus plain `man`). Completions are attempted in the following order, based on the options provided to the `complete` command:

1. If completion is attempted on an empty input line, Bash applies the compspec given with `complete -E`. Otherwise, it proceeds to the next step.

2. Bash first identifies the command. If a pathname is used, Bash looks to see if a compspec exists for the full pathname. Otherwise, it sets the command name to the last component of the pathname, and searches for a compspec for the command name.

3. If a compspec exists, Bash uses it. If not, Bash uses the "default" compspec given with `complete -D`. If there is none, then Bash falls back to the default built-in completions.

4. Bash performs the action indicated by the compspec to generate a list of possible matches. Of this list, only those that have the word being completed as a prefix are used for the list of possible completions. For the `-d` and `-f` options, the variable `FIGNORE` is used to filter out undesirable matches.

5. Bash generates filenames as specified by the `-G` option. `GLOBIGNORE` is not used to filter the results, but `FIGNORE` is.

6. Bash processes the argument string provided to `-W`. The string is split using the characters in `$IFS`. The resulting list provides the candidates for completion. This is often used to provide a list of options that a command accepts.

7. Bash runs functions and commands as specified by the `-F` and `-C` options. For both, Bash sets `COMP_LINE` and `COMP_POINT` as described in the section "Built-in Shell Variables" on page 24. For a shell function, `COMP_WORDS` and `COMP_CWORD` are also set.

   Also, for both functions and commands, `$1` is the name of the command whose arguments are being completed, `$2` is the word being completed, and `$3` is the word in front of the word being completed. Bash does *not* filter the results of the command or function:

   a. Functions named with `-F` are run first. The function should set the `COMPREPLY` array to the list of possible completions. Bash retrieves the list from there.

   b. Commands provided with `-C` are run next, in an environment equivalent to command substitution.

The command should print the list of possible completions, one per line. An embedded newline should be escaped with a backslash.

8. Once the list is generated, Bash filters the results according to the -X option. The argument to -X is a pattern specifying files to exclude. By prefixing the pattern with a !, the sense is reversed, and the pattern instead specifies that only matching files should be retained in the list.

   An & in the pattern is replaced with the text of the word being completed. Use \& to produce a literal &.

9. Finally, Bash prepends or appends any prefixes or suffixes supplied with the -P or -S options.

10. In the case that no matches were generated, if -o dirnames was used, Bash attempts directory name completion.

11. On the other hand, if -o plusdirs was provided, Bash *adds* the result of directory completion to the previously generated list.

12. Normally, when a compspec is provided, Bash's default completions are not attempted, nor are the *readline* library's default filename completions:

    a. If the compspec produces no results and -o bashdefault was provided, then Bash attempts its default completions.

    b. If neither the compspec nor the Bash default completions with -o bashdefault produced any results, and -o default was provided, then Bash has the *readline* library attempt its filename completions.

A compspec may be modified with the compopt command. When used without command names inside an executing completion, it affects the executing completion.

When a shell function used as a completion handler returns 124, Bash retries the completion process from the beginning. This is most useful with the default completion handler (complete -D) to dynamically build up a set of completions instead of loading a large set at startup. The *bash*(1) manpage has an example at the end of its Programmable Completion section.

Ian Macdonald has collected a large set of useful compspecs, often distributed as the file **/etc/bash_completion**. If your system does not have it, you can download it at *http://freshmeat .net/projects/bashcompletion/*. It is worth reviewing.

Examples

Restrict files for the C compiler to C, C++ and assembler source files, and relocatable object files:

```
complete -f -X '!*.[Ccos]' gcc cc
```

For the man command, restrict expansions to things that have manpages:

```
# Simple example of programmable completion for manual pages.
# A more elaborate example appears in bash_completion file.
# Assumes    man [num] command    command syntax.

shopt -s extglob    # Enable extended pattern matching

# Define completion function
_man () {
 local dir mandir=/usr/share/man          # Local variables

 COMPREPLY=( )                            # Clear reply list
 if [[ ${COMP_WORDS[1]} = +([0-9]) ]]     # Have section no.
 then
     # section provided: man 3 foo
     # look in specified directory
     dir=$mandir/man${COMP_WORDS[COMP_CWORD-1]}
 else
     # no section, default to commands
     # look in command directories
     dir=$mandir/'man[18]'
 fi
 COMPREPLY=( $(
   # Generate raw file list
   find $dir -type f |
```

```
        # Remove leading directories
        sed 's;..*/;;' |

            # Remove trailing suffixes
            sed 's/\.[0-9].*$//' |

                # Keep those that match given prefix
                grep "^${COMP_WORDS[$COMP_CWORD]}" |

                    # Sort final list
                    sort
    ) )
}

# Associate function with command
complete -F _man man
```

Job Control

Job control lets you place foreground jobs in the background, bring background jobs to the foreground, or suspend running jobs. All modern Unix systems—including Mac OS X, GNU/Linux and BSD systems—support it, so the job control features are automatically enabled. Many job control commands take a *jobID* as an argument, which can be specified as follows:

%*n*   Job number *n*

%*s*   Job whose command line starts with string *s*

%?*s*   Job whose command line contains string *s*

%%   Current job

%+   Current job (same as above)

%   Current job (same as above)

%-   Previous job

The shell provides the following job control commands. For more information on these commands, see the section "Built-in Commands" on page 55.

bg
> Put the current job in the background.

fg
> Put the current job in the foreground.

jobs
> List active jobs.

kill
> Terminate a job.

stty tostop
> Stop background jobs if they try to send output to the terminal. (Note that **stty** is not a built-in command.)

suspend
> Suspend a job-control shell (such as one created by **su**).

wait
> Wait for background jobs to finish.

CTRL-Z
> Suspend a foreground job. Then use **bg** or **fg**. (Your terminal may use something other than **CTRL-Z** as the suspend character, but this is unlikely.)

Shell Options

Bash provides a number of shell options, settings that you can change to modify the shell's behavior. You control these options with the **shopt** command (see the entry for **shopt** on page 98). The following descriptions describe the behavior when set. Options marked with a dagger (†) are enabled by default:

autocd
> When the first word of a simple command cannot be executed, try to **cd** to it.

cdable_vars
> Treat a nondirectory argument to **cd** as a variable whose value is the directory to go to.

cdspell

Attempt spelling correction on each directory component of an argument to **cd**. Allowed in interactive shells only.

checkhash

Check that commands found in the hash table still exist before attempting to use them. If not, perform a normal **PATH** search.

checkjobs

When an attempt is made to exit a shell and there are stopped or running background jobs, the shell prints **There are running jobs.** and a list of jobs and their statuses. A second exit attempt (such as typing *EOF* again) causes the shell to exit.

checkwinsize

Check the window size after each command, and update **LINES** and **COLUMNS** if the size has changed.

cmdhist †

Save all lines of a multiline command in one history entry. This permits easy re-editing of multiline commands.

compat31

Mutually exclusive with the **compat32** and **compat40** options. Restore the behavior of the =~ operator for the [[ ]] command whereby the righthand side is always treated as a regular expression to be matched. In addition, the < and > operators ignore the locale when doing string comparison.

compat32

Mutually exclusive with the **compat31** and **compat40** options. Cause the < and > operators of the [[ ]] command to ignore the locale when doing string comparison.

compat40

Mutually exclusive with the **compat31** and **compat32** options. Cause the < and > operators of the [[ ]] command to ignore the locale when doing string comparison. In addition, interrupting a command list such as **cmd1; cmd2; cmd3** aborts execution of the entire list. (Prior to version 4.0, interrupting one command in a list did not prevent the following commands from executing.)

dirspell

Attempt spelling correction on directory names during word completion if the name as given does not exist.

dotglob

Include filenames starting with a period in the results of filename expansion.

execfail

Do not exit a noninteractive shell if the command given to **exec** cannot be executed. Interactive shells do not exit in such a case, no matter the setting of this option.

expand_aliases †

Expand aliases created with **alias**. Disabled in noninteractive shells.

extdebug

Enable behavior needed for debuggers:

- **declare** -F displays the source filename and line number for each function name argument.
- When a command run by the **DEBUG** trap fails, the next command is skipped.
- When a command run by the **DEBUG** trap inside a shell function or script sourced with . (dot) or **source** returns with an exit status of 2, the shell simulates a call to **return**.
- **BASH_ARGC** and **BASH_ARGV** are set as described earlier.
- Function tracing is enabled. Command substitutions, shell functions, and subshells invoked via (...) inherit the **DEBUG** and **RETURN** traps.
- Error tracing is enabled. Command substitutions, shell functions, and subshells invoked via (...) inherit the **ERR** trap.

extglob

Enable extended pattern-matching facilities such as +(...). (These were not in the Bourne shell and are not in POSIX; thus Bash requires you to enable them if you want them.)

extquote †

Allow $'...' and $"..." within ${*variable*} expansions inside double quotes.

failglob

Cause patterns that do not match filenames to produce an error.

force_fignore †

When doing completion, ignore words matching the list of suffixes in FIGNORE, even if such words are the only possible completions.

globstar †

Enable extended directory and subdirectory matching with the special ** pattern.

gnu_errfmt

Print error messages in the standard GNU format. Enabled automatically when Bash runs in an Emacs terminal window.

histappend

Append the history list to the file named by $HISTFILE upon exit, instead of overwriting the file.

histreedit

Allow a user to re-edit a failed csh-style history substitution with the *readline* library.

histverify

Place the results of csh-style history substitution into the *readline* library's editing buffer instead of executing it directly, in case the user wishes to modify it further.

hostcomplete †

If using *readline*, attempt hostname completion when a word containing an @ is being completed.

---

huponexit

Send a `SIGHUP` to all running jobs upon exiting an interactive login shell.

interactive_comments †

Allow words beginning with `#` to start a comment in an interactive shell.

lithist

If `cmdhist` is also set, save multiline commands to the history file with newlines instead of semicolons.

login_shell

Set by the shell when it is a login shell. This is a read-only option.

mailwarn

Print the message `The mail in` *mailfile* `has been read` when a file being checked for mail has been accessed since the last time Bash checked it.

no_empty_cmd_completion

If using *readline*, do *not* search `$PATH` when a completion is attempted on an empty line, or a line consisting solely of whitespace.

nocaseglob

Ignore letter case when doing filename matching.

nocasematch

Ignore letter case when doing pattern matching for `case` and `[[ ]]`.

nullglob

Expand patterns that do not match any files to the null string, instead of using the literal pattern as an argument.

progcomp †

Enable programmable completion.

promptvars †

Perform variable, command, and arithmetic substitution on the values of `PS1`, `PS2`, and `PS4`.

restricted_shell

> Set by the shell when it is a restricted shell. This is a read-only option.

shift_verbose

> Causes `shift` to print an error message when the shift count is greater than the number of positional parameters.

sourcepath †

> Causes the `.` (dot) and `source` commands to search `$PATH` in order to find the file to read and execute.

xpg_echo

> Causes `echo` to expand escape sequences, even without the `-e` or `-E` options.

Command Execution

When you type a command, Bash looks in the following places until it finds a match:

1. Keywords such as `if` and `for`.

2. Aliases. You can't define an alias whose name is a shell keyword, but you can define an alias that expands to a keyword, e.g., `alias aslongas=while`. When not in POSIX mode, Bash does allow you to define an alias for a shell keyword.

3. Special built-ins like `break` and `continue`. The list of POSIX special built-ins is `.` (dot), `:`, `break`, `continue`, `eval`, `exec`, `exit`, `export`, `readonly`, `return`, `set`, `shift`, `times`, `trap`, and `unset`. Bash adds `source`.

4. Functions. When not in POSIX mode, Bash finds functions before all built-in commands.

5. Nonspecial built-ins such as `cd` and `test`.

6. Scripts and executable programs, for which the shell searches in the directories listed in the `PATH` environment variable.

7. When a command is not found, if a function named `command_not_found_handle` exists, the shell will call it, passing the command words as the function arguments.

The distinction between "special" built-in commands and non-special ones comes from POSIX. This distinction, combined with the `command` command, makes it possible to write functions that override shell built-ins, such as `cd`. For example:

```
cd () {                          Shell function; found before built-in cd
    command cd "$@"              Use real cd to change directory
    echo now in $PWD            Other stuff we want to do
}
```

If Bash exits due to receiving `SIGHUP`, or if the `huponexit` shell option is set, Bash will send a `SIGHUP` to all running child jobs. Use `disown -h` to prevent Bash from sending `SIGHUP` to a particular job.

Coprocesses

A *coprocess* is a process that runs in parallel with the shell and with which the shell can communicate. The shell starts the process in the background, connecting its standard input and output to a two-way pipe. There are two syntaxes for running a coprocess:

`coproc name non-simple command`   Start a named coprocess

`coproc command args`   Start an unnamed coprocess

The shell creates an array variable named *name* to hold the file descriptors for communication with the coprocess. *name*[0] is the output of the coprocess (input to the controlling shell) and *name*[1] is the input to the coprocess (output from the shell). In addition, the variable *name*_PID holds the process-ID of the coprocess. When no name is supplied, the shell uses `COPROC`.

Example

The following example demonstrates the basic usage of the
coproc keyword and the related variables:

```
$ coproc testproc (echo 1              Start a named coprocess
> read aline ; echo $aline)            in the background
[1] 5090
$ echo ${testproc[@]}                  Show the file descriptors
63 60
$ echo $testproc_PID                   Show the coprocess PID
5090
$ read out <&${testproc[0]}            Read the first line of coprocess
$ echo $out                            output and show it
1
$ echo foo >&${testproc[1]}            Send coprocess some input
$ read out2 <&${testproc[0]}           Read second output line
[1]+ Done  coproc testproc (echo 1; read aline; echo $aline)
$ echo $out2                           Show the second output line
foo
```

Restricted Shells

A *restricted shell* is one that disallows certain actions, such as
changing directory, setting PATH, or running commands whose
names contain a / character.

The original V7 Bourne shell had an undocumented restricted
mode. Later versions of the Bourne shell clarified the code and
documented the facility. Bash also supplies a restricted mode.
(See the manual page for the details.)

Shell scripts can still be run, since in that case the restricted
shell calls the unrestricted version of the shell to run the script.
This includes /etc/profile, $HOME/.profile, and the other
startup files.

Restricted shells are not used much in practice, as they are difficult to set up correctly.

Built-in Commands

Examples to be entered as a command line are shown with the $ prompt. Otherwise, examples should be treated as code fragments that might be included in a shell script. For convenience, some of the reserved words used by multiline commands are also included.

!   Invert the sense of the following pipeline.

`! pipeline`

Negate the sense of a pipeline. Returns an exit status of 0 if the pipeline exited nonzero, and an exit status of 1 if the pipeline exited zero. Typically used in `if` and `while` statements.

Example

This code prints a message if user `jane` is not logged on:

```
if ! who | grep jane > /dev/null
then
    echo jane is not currently logged on
fi
```

Introduce a comment that runs to the end of the line.

`# text …`

Ignore all text that follows on the same line. # is used in shell scripts as the comment character and is not really a command.

#!shell — Invoke the named interpreter to execute the script.

`#!shell [option]`

Used as the first line of a script to invoke the named *shell*. Anything given on the rest of the line is passed *as a single argument* to the named *shell*. This feature is typically implemented by the kernel, but may not be supported on some very old systems. Some systems have a limit of around 32 characters on the maximum length of *shell*. For example:

```
#!/bin/sh
```

: — Do-nothing command, used as a syntactic placeholder.

`: [arguments]`

Null command. Returns an exit status of 0. See this Example and the ones under `case` on page 60. The line is still processed for side effects, such as variable and command substitutions, or I/O redirection.

Example

Check whether someone is logged in:

```
if who | grep $1 > /dev/null
then :    # Do nothing if user is found
else echo "User $1 is not logged in"
fi
```

. — Read and execute a file within the current shell.

`. file [arguments]`

Read and execute lines in *file*. *file* does not have to be executable but must reside in a directory searched by $PATH. If the sourcepath option is not enabled, Bash does not search $PATH. The *arguments* are stored in the positional parameters. If Bash is not in POSIX mode and *file* is not found in $PATH, Bash looks in the current directory for *file*. Bash removes NUL bytes from the contents of *file* before attempting to parse it. See also `source` on page 99.

[[ ]]   **Extended version of the test command.**

`[[ expression ]]`

Same as **test** *expression* or [*expression*], except that [[ ]] allows additional operators. Word splitting and filename expansion are disabled. Note that the brackets ([ ]) are typed literally, and that they must be surrounded by whitespace. See **test** on page 99.

Additional Operators

&& Logical AND of test expressions (short circuit).

|| Logical OR of test expressions (short circuit).

< First string is lexically "less than" the second, based on the locale's sorting order. (However, see the description of the com pat31, compat32, and compat40 options in the section "Shell Options" on page 47.)

> First string is lexically "greater than" the second, based on the locale's sorting order. (However, see the description of the com pat31, compat32, and compat40 options in the section "Shell Options" on page 47.)

name ()   **Define a shell function.**

`name () { commands; } [redirections]`

Define *name* as a function. POSIX syntax. The function definition can be written on one line or across many. You may also provide the **function** keyword, an alternate form that works similarly. See the section "Functions" on page 18.

Example

```
$ countfiles () {
>     ls | wc -l
> }
```

When issued at the command line, countfiles now displays the number of files in the current directory.

alias   **Define and manage shell aliases.**

```
alias [-p] [name[='cmd']]
```

Assign a shorthand *name* as a synonym for *cmd*. If =*'cmd'* is omitted, print the alias for *name*; if *name* is also omitted, print all aliases. If the alias value contains a trailing space, the next word on the command line also becomes a candidate for alias expansion. The BASH_ALIASES array provides programmatic access to all defined aliases; see the section "Built-in Shell Variables" on page 24. See also unalias on page 107.

Option

-p
> Print the word alias before each alias.

Example

```
alias dir='echo ${PWD##*/}'
```

---

bg   **Move a stopped job into the background.**

```
bg [jobIDs]
```

Put current job or *jobIDs* in the background. See the section "Job Control" on page 46.

---

bind   **Manage key bindings for the *readline* library.**

```
bind [-m map] [options]
bind [-m map] [-q function] [-r sequence] [-u function]
bind [-m map] -f file
bind [-m map] -x sequence:command
bind [-m map]  sequence:function
bind readline-command
```

Manage the *readline* library. Nonoption arguments have the same form as in a .inputrc file.

Options

-f *file*
> Read key bindings from *file*.

-l

List the names of all the *readline* functions.

-m *map*

Use *map* as the keymap. Available keymaps are emacs, emacs-ctlx, emacs-standard, emacs-meta, vi, vi-command, vi-insert, and vi-move. vi is the same as vi-command, and emacs is the same as emacs-standard.

-p

Print the current *readline* bindings such that they can be reread from a .inputrc file.

-P

Print the current *readline* bindings.

-q *function*

Query which keys invoke the *readline* function *function*.

-r *sequence*

Remove the binding for key sequence *sequence*.

-s

Print the current *readline* key sequence and macro bindings such that they can be reread from a .inputrc file.

-S

Print the current *readline* key sequence and macro bindings.

-u *function*

Unbind all keys that invoke the *readline* function *function*.

-v

Print the current *readline* variables such that they can be reread from a .inputrc file.

-V

Print the current *readline* variables.

-x *sequence:command*

Execute the shell command *command* whenever *sequence* is entered. The *command* may make use of and modify the READ LINE_LINE and READLINE_POINT variables. Changes to these variables are reflected in the editing state.

break
Exit from one or more loops.

```
break [n]
```

Exit from a for, while, select, or until loop (or break out of *n* nested loops).

builtin
Execute a built-in command, bypassing functions.

```
builtin command [arguments …]
```

Run the shell built-in command *command* with the given arguments. This allows you to bypass any functions that redefine a built-in command's name. The command command is more portable.

Example

This function lets you do your own tasks when you change directory:

```
cd () {
    builtin cd "$@"              Actually change directory
    pwd                         Report location
}
```

caller
Print function or dot-file caller, for use with the Bash debugger.

```
caller [expression]
```

Print the line number and source filename of the current function call or dot file. With nonzero *expression*, print that element from the call stack. The most recent is zero. This command is for use by the Bash debugger.

case
Syntax for a case statement.

```
case value in
  pattern1) cmds1;;     # ;& or ;;& -- see text
  pattern2) cmds2;;
    . . .
esac
```

Execute the first set of commands (*cmds1*) if *value* matches *pattern1*, execute the second set of commands (*cmds2*) if *value* matches *pattern2*, etc. Be sure the last command in each set ends with ;;. *value* is typically a positional parameter or other shell variable. *cmds* are typically Unix commands, shell programming commands, or variable assignments. Patterns can use file-generation metacharacters. Multiple patterns (separated by |) can be specified on the same line; in this case, the associated *cmds* are executed whenever *value* matches any of these patterns. See the Examples here and under eval on page 73.

The shell allows *pattern* to be preceded by an optional open parenthesis, as in (*pattern*). For some shell versions, it's necessary for balancing parentheses inside a $( ) construct. Bash 4.0 and 4.1 do not require it. See also the nocasematch option in "Shell Options" on page 47.

Bash provides two additional special terminators for the *cmds* in a case statement. ;& causes execution to continue into the next set of *cmds*. ;;& causes the next *pattern* list to be tested.

Examples

Check first command-line argument and take appropriate action:

```
case $1 in       # Match the first arg
no|yes) response=1;;
-[tT])  table=TRUE;;
*)      echo "unknown option"; exit 1;;
esac
```

Read user-supplied lines until user exits:

```
while :          # Null command; always true
do     printf "Type . to finish ==> "
       read line
       case "$line" in
       .)  echo "Message done"
           break ;;
       *)  echo "$line" >> $message ;;
       esac
done
```

cd

```
cd [-LP] [dir]
cd [-LP] [-]
```

With no arguments, change to home directory of user. Otherwise, change working directory to *dir*. Bash searches the directories given in $CDPATH first, and then looks in the current directory for *dir*. If *dir* is a relative pathname but is not in the current directory, then $CDPATH is also searched. A directory of - stands for the previous directory.

Options

-L

Use the logical path (what the user typed, including any symbolic links) for cd .. and the value of PWD. This is the default.

-P

Use the filesystem physical path for cd .. and the value of PWD.

Example

```
$ ls -ld /usr/tmp              /usr/tmp is a symbolic link
lrwxrwxrwx 1 root root 10 Dec 26 2008 /usr/tmp ->../var/tmp
$ cd -L /usr/tmp               Logical change directory
$ pwd                          Show location
/usr/tmp                       Result is logical location
$ cd -P /usr/tmp               Physical change directory
$ pwd                          Show location
/var/tmp                       Result is physical location
```

command

```
command [-pvV] name [arg …]
```

Without -v or -V, execute *name* with given arguments. This command bypasses any aliases or functions that may be defined for *name*. When used with a special built-in, it prevents the built-in from exiting the script if it fails.

Options

-p

Use a predefined default search path, not the current value of
PATH.

-v

Print a description of how the shell interprets *name*.

-V

Print a more verbose description of how the shell interprets
name.

Example

Create an alias for rm that will get the system's version, and run it
with the -i option:

```
$ alias 'rm=command -p rm -i'
```

---

compgen   Generate possible completions.

compgen [*options*] [*string*]

Generate possible completions for *string* according to the options.
Options are those accepted by complete, except for -p and -r. For
more information, see the entry for complete on page 63.

---

complete   Specify how to do completion for specific commands.

complete [-DE] [*options*] *command* ...

Specifies the way to complete arguments for each *command*. This
is discussed in the section "Programmable Completion"
on page 41.

Options

-a

Same as -A alias.

-A *type*

Use *type* to specify a list of possible completions. The *type* may
be one of the following:

alias	Alias names
arrayvar	Array variable names
binding	Bindings from the *readline* library
builtin	Shell built-in command names
command	Command names
directory	Directory names
disabled	Names of disabled shell built-in commands
enabled	Names of enabled shell built-in commands
export	Exported variables
file	Filenames
function	Names of shell functions
group	Group names
helptopic	Help topics as allowed by the help built-in command
hostname	Hostnames, as found in the file named by $HOSTFILE
job	Job names
keyword	Shell reserved keywords
running	Names of running jobs
service	Service names (from /etc/services)
setopt	Valid arguments for set -o
shopt	Valid option names for the shopt built-in command
signal	Signal names
stopped	Names of stopped jobs
user	Usernames
variable	Shell variable names

-b

Same as -A builtin.

-c

Same as -A command.

-C *command*

Run *command* in a subshell and use its output as the list of completions.

-d

Same as `-A directory`.

-D

Apply the rest of the options and parameters to the "default" completion, which is used when no other compspec can be found.

-e

Same as `-A export`.

-E

Apply the rest of the options and parameters to the "empty" completion, which is used when completion is attempted on an empty input line.

-f

Same as `-A file`.

-F *function*

Run shell function *function* in the current shell. Upon its return, retrieve the list of completions from the `COMPREPLY` array.

-g

Same as `-A group`.

-G *pattern*

Expand *pattern* to generate completions.

-j

Same as `-A job`.

-k

Same as `-A keyword`.

-o *option*

Control the behavior of the completion specification. The value for *option* is one of the following:

bashdefault	Fall back to the normal Bash completions if no matches are produced.
default	Use the default *readline* completions if no matches are produced.
dirnames	Do directory name completion if no matches are produced.

filenames	Inform the *readline* library that the intended output is filenames, so the library can do any filename-specific processing, such as adding a trailing slash for directories or removing trailing spaces.
nospace	Inform the *readline* library that it should not append a space to words completed at the end of a line.
plusdirs	Attempt directory completion and add any results to the list of completions already generated.

-p

With no commands, print all completion settings in a way that can be reread.

-P *prefix*

Prepend *prefix* to each resulting string after all the other options have been applied.

-r

Remove the completion settings for the given commands, or all settings if no commands.

-s

Same as -A service.

-S *suffix*

Append *suffix* to each resulting string after all the other options have been applied.

-u

Same as -A user.

-v

Same as -A variable.

-W *wordlist*

Split *wordlist* (a single shell word) using $IFS. The generated list contains the members of the split list that matched the word being completed. Each member is expanded using brace expansion, tilde expansion, parameter and variable expansion, command substitution, and arithmetic expansion. Shell quoting is respected.

`-X` *pattern*

> Exclude filenames matching *pattern* from the filename completion list. With a leading !, the sense is reversed, and only filenames matching *pattern* are retained.

---

compopt   Print or change the completion options for a command.

`compopt [-DE] [-o options] [+o options] [command …]`

With no options, print the completion options for *commands* or for the currently executing completion when invoked without *commands*. With options, modify the existing compspecs for the given *commands*, or for the currently executing completion when invoked without *commands*.

Options

`-D`

> Apply the *options* to the "default" completion.

`-E`

> Apply the *options* to the "empty" completion.

`-o` *option*

> Enable *option*, which is one of the valid options for the `complete` command.

`+o` *option*

> Disable *option*, which is one of the valid options for the `complete` command.

---

continue   Skip the rest of the body of one or more loops.

`continue [n]`

Skip remaining commands in a `for`, `while`, `select`, or `until` loop, resuming with the next iteration of the loop (or skipping *n* nested loops).

declare

```
declare [options] [name[=value]]
```

Declare variables and manage their attributes. In function bodies, variables are local, as if declared with the `local` command. All options must be given first. See also **typeset** on page 105.

Options

-a

Each *name* is an indexed array.

-A

Each *name* is an associative array.

-f

Each *name* is a function.

-F

For functions, print just the function's name and attributes, not the function definition (body).

-i

Each variable is an integer; in an assignment, the value is evaluated as an arithmetic expression.

-l

Mark *names* to have their values converted to lower case upon assignment.

-p

With no *names*, print all variables, their values, and attributes. With *names*, print the names, attributes, and values of the given variables. With `-f`, print function values and attributes.

-r

Mark *names* as read-only. Subsequent assignments will fail, and read-only variables cannot be unset.

-t

Apply the *trace* attribute to each name. Traced functions inherit the DEBUG trap. This attribute has no meaning for variables.

-u

> Mark *names* to have their values converted to upper case upon assignment.

-x

> Mark *names* for export into the environment of child processes.

With a + instead of a -, the given attribute is disabled. With no variable names, all variables having the given attribute(s) are printed in a form that can be reread as input to the shell.

Examples

```
$ declare -i val              Make val an integer
$ val=4+7                     Evaluate value
$ echo $val                   Show result
11

$ declare -r z=42            Make z read-only
$ z=31                       Try to assign to it
bash: z: readonly variable   Assignment fails
$ echo $z
42

$ declare -p val z            Show attributes and values
declare -i val="11"
declare -r z="42"
```

---

dirs   Print or manage the directory stack.

`dirs [-clpv] [+n] [-n]`

Print the directory stack, which is managed with pushd and popd.

Options

+*n*

> Print the *n*th entry from the left; first entry is zero.

-*n*

> Print the *n*th entry from the right; first entry is zero.

-c

> Remove all entries from (clear) the directory stack.

-l

> Produce a longer listing, one that does not replace $HOME with
> ~.

-p

> Print the directory stack, one entry per line.

-v

> Print the directory stack, one entry per line, with each entry
> preceded by its index in the stack.

---

disown   Stop managing one or more jobs.

disown [-ahr] [*job* …]

Remove *jobs* from the list of jobs managed by Bash.

Options

-a

> Remove all jobs. With -h, mark all jobs.

-h

> Instead of removing jobs from the list of known jobs, mark
> them to *not* receive SIGHUP as described in the section "Com-
> mand Execution" on page 52.

-r

> With no jobs, remove (or mark) only running jobs.

---

do   Reserved word that starts the body of a loop.

do

Reserved word that precedes the command sequence in a for, while,
until, or select statement.

---

done   Reserved word that ends the body of a loop.

done

Reserved word that ends a for, while, until, or select statement.

---

echo   **Print command-line arguments to standard output.**

```
echo [-eEn] [string]
```

Built-in version. Write *string* to standard output.

Options

If the xpg_echo shell option is set, along with POSIX mode (set -o posix), echo does not interpret any options.

-e

> Enable interpretation of the following escape sequences, which must be quoted (or escaped with a \\) to prevent interpretation by the shell:

> \\a
>> Alert (ASCII BEL).

> \\b
>> Backspace.

> \\c
>> Suppress the terminating newline (same as -n).

> \\e
>> ASCII Escape character.

> \\f
>> Formfeed.

> \\n
>> Newline.

> \\r
>> Carriage return.

> \\t
>> Tab character.

> \\v
>> Vertical-tab character.

> \\\\
>> Backslash.

\0*nnn*

> ASCII character represented by octal number *nnn*, where *nnn* is zero, one, two, or three digits and is preceded by a 0.

\x*HH*

> ASCII character represented by hexadecimal number *HH*, where *HH* is one or two hexadecimal digits.

-E

> Do not interpret escape sequences, even on systems where the default behavior of the built-in echo is to interpret them.

-n

> Do not print the terminating newline.

Examples

```
$ echo "testing printer" | lp
$ echo "Warning: ringing bell \a"
```

---

enable   Enable or disable shell built-in commands.

```
enable [-adnps] [-f file] [command ...]
```

Enable or disable shell built-in commands. Disabling a built-in lets you use an external version of a command that would otherwise use a built-in version, such as echo or test.

Options

-a

> For use with -p; print information about all built-in commands, disabled and enabled.

-d

> Remove (delete) a built-in previously loaded with -f.

-f *file*

> Load a new built-in command *command* from the shared library file *file*.

-n

> Disable the named built-in commands.

-p

Print a list of enabled built-in commands.

-s

Print only the POSIX special built-in commands. When combined with -f, the new built-in command becomes a POSIX special built-in.

---

esac   Reserved word that ends a case statement.

esac

Reserved word that ends a case statement.

---

eval   Rescan and execute an already-processed input line.

eval *args*

Typically, eval is used in shell scripts, and *args* is a line of code that contains shell variables. eval forces variable expansion to happen first and then runs the resulting command. This "double-scanning" is useful any time shell variables contain input/output redirection symbols, aliases, or other shell variables. (For example, redirection normally happens before variable expansion, so a variable containing redirection symbols must be expanded first using eval; otherwise, the redirection symbols remain uninterpreted.)

Example

This fragment of a shell script shows how eval constructs a command that is interpreted in the right order:

```
for option
do
    case "$option" in                Define where output goes
    save) out=' > $newfile' ;;
    show) out=' | more' ;;
    esac
done

eval sort $file $out
```

exec   Replace the current script or manage shell file descriptors.

```
exec [command args …]
exec [-a name] [-cl] [command args … ]
exec redirections …
```

Execute *command* in place of the current process (instead of creating a new process). With only redirections, **exec** is also useful for opening, closing, copying, or moving file descriptors. In this case, the script continues to run.

Options

-a

> Use *name* for the value of **argv[0]**.

-c

> Clear the environment before executing the program.

-l

> Place a minus sign at the front of **argv[0]**, just as *login*(1) does.

Examples

```
trap 'exec 2>&-' 0        Close stderr when script exits (signal 0)
```

```
$ exec /bin/csh           Replace shell with C shell
$ exec < infile           Reassign standard input to infile
```

exit   Exit the shell script.

```
exit [n]
```

Exit a shell script with status *n* (e.g., **exit 1**). *n* can be 0 (success) or nonzero (failure). If *n* is not given, the shell's exit status is that of the most recent command. **exit** can be issued at the command line to close a window (log out). Exit statuses can range in value from 0 to 255. Any trap on **EXIT** is executed before the shell exits.

Example

```
if [ $# -eq 0 ]
then
    echo "Usage: $0 [-c] [-d] file(s)" 1>&2
    exit 1                 # Error status
fi
```

export
Export variables or print information about exported variables.

```
export [variables]
export [name=[value] …]
export -p
export [-fn] [name=[value] …]
```

Pass (export) the value of one or more shell *variables*, giving global meaning to the variables (which are local by default). For example, a variable defined in one shell script must be exported if its value is used in other programs called by the script. If no *variables* are given, **export** lists the variables exported by the current shell. The second form is the POSIX version, which is similar to the first form, except that you can set a variable *name* to a *value* before exporting it.

Options

-f

Names refer to functions; the functions are exported in the environment.

-n

Remove the named variables or functions from the environment.

-p

Print **export** before printing the names and values of exported variables. This allows saving a list of exported variables for rereading later.

Examples

In the original Bourne shell, you would type:

```
TERM=vt100
export TERM
```

In Bash, you could type this instead:

```
export TERM=vt100
```

false
Exit with a false return value.

```
false
```

Built-in command that exits with a false return value.

```
fc [options] [first [last]]
fc -e - [old=new] [command]
fc -s [old=new] [command]
```

Display or edit commands in the history list. (Use only one of -e, -1, or -s.) *first* and *last* are numbers or strings specifying the range of commands to display or edit. If *last* is omitted, fc applies to a single command (specified by *first*). If both *first* and *last* are omitted, fc edits the previous command or lists the last 16. The second form of fc takes a history *command*, replaces *old* with *new*, and executes the modified command. If no strings are specified, *command* is just re-executed. If no *command* is given either, the previous command is re-executed. *command* is a number or string like *first*. See the Examples in the section "Command History" on page 37. The third form is equivalent to the second form.

Options

-e *[editor]*

> Invoke *editor* to edit the specified history commands. The default *editor* is set by the shell variable FCEDIT. If that variable is not set, the default is /bin/ed. (Bash defaults to vi; versions 3.1 and newer default to /bin/ed when in POSIX mode.) Bash tries $FCEDIT, then $EDITOR, and then /bin/ed.

-e -

> Execute (or redo) a history command; refer to second syntax line above.

-1

> List the specified command or range of commands, or list the last 16.

-n

> Suppress command numbering from the -1 listing.

-r

> Reverse the order of the -1 listing.

-s

> Equivalent to -e -.

fg   Move a running or suspended background job into the foreground.

fg [*jobIDs*]

Bring current job or *jobIDs* to the foreground. See the section "Job Control" on page 46.

---

fi   Reserved word that ends an if statement.

fi

Reserved word that ends an if statement.

---

for   Start a loop over a list of values.

```
for x [in [list]]
do
    commands
done
```

For variable *x* (in optional *list* of values), do *commands*. If in *list* is omitted, "$@" (the positional parameters) is assumed. If the expansion of *list* is empty, no *commands* are executed.

Examples

Paginate files specified on the command line, and save each result:

```
for file
do
    pr $file > $file.tmp
done
```

Same, but put entire loop into the background:

```
for file
do
    pr $file > $file.tmp
done &
```

Search chapters for a list of words (like fgrep -f):

```
for item in `cat program_list`
do
    echo "Checking chapters for"
    echo "references to program $item…"
```

```
    grep -c "$item.[co]" chap*
done
```

Extract a one-word title from each file named on the command line and use it as the new filename:

```
for file
do
    name=`sed -n 's/NAME: //p' $file`
    mv $file $name
done
```

---

for   Start an arithmetic loop.

```
for ((init; cond; incr))
do
    commands
done
```

Arithmetic **for** loop, similar to C's. Evaluate *init*. While *cond* is true, execute the body of the loop. Evaluate *incr* before retesting *cond*. Any one of the expressions may be omitted; a missing *cond* is treated as being true.

Example

Search for a phrase in each odd chapter:

```
for ((x=1; x <= 20; x += 2))
do
    grep $1 chap$x
done
```

---

function   Define a shell function.

```
function name { commands; } [redirections]
function name () { commands; } [redirections]
```

Define *name* as a shell function. See the description of function semantics in the section "Functions" on page 18.

Example

Define a function to count files.

```
$ function countfiles {
>     ls | wc -l
> }
```

---

getopts   Process command-line options and arguments.

getopts *string name* [*args*]

Process command-line arguments (or *args*, if specified) and check
for legal options. getopts is used in shell script loops and is intended
to ensure standard syntax for command-line options. Standard syntax dictates that command-line options begin with a -. Options can
be stacked; i.e., consecutive letters can follow a single -. End processing of options by specifying -- on the command line. *string*
contains the option letters to be recognized by getopts when running the shell script. Valid options are processed in turn and stored
in the shell variable *name*. If an option character in the options string
is followed by a colon, the actual option must be followed by one
or more arguments. (Multiple arguments must be given to the command as one shell *word*. This is done by quoting the arguments or
separating them with commas. The application must be written to
expect multiple arguments in this format.) getopts uses the shell
variables OPTARG, OPTIND, and OPTERR.

---

hash   Manage the table of previously found commands.

hash [-dlrt] [-p *file*] [*commands*]

As the shell finds commands along the search path ($PATH), it re-
members the found locations in an internal hash table. The next
time you enter a command, the shell uses the value stored in its hash
table.

With no arguments, hash lists the current hashed commands. The
display shows *hits* (the number of times the command has been
called by the shell) and the command name. If the table is empty,
then if Bash is in POSIX mode, hash prints nothing. Otherwise, it
prints hash: hash table empty on standard output.

With *commands*, the shell adds those commands to the hash table. With no options and just *commands*, the shell resets the "hit count" associated with each command to zero.

The BASH_CMDS array provides programmatic access to all entries in the hash table; see the section "Built-in Shell Variables" on page 24.

Options

-d

    Remove (delete) just the specified commands from the hash table.

-l

    Produce output in a format that can be reread to rebuild the hash table.

-p *file*
    Associate *file* with *command* in the hash table.

-r

    Remove all commands from the hash table.

-t

    With one name, print the full pathname of the command. With more than one name, print the name and the full path, in two columns.

Besides the -r option, the hash table is also cleared when PATH is assigned. Use PATH=$PATH to clear the hash table without affecting your search path. This is most useful if you have installed a new version of a command in a directory that is earlier in $PATH than the current version of the command.

---

help   Print command usage information.

help [-dms] [*pattern*]

Print usage information on standard output for each command that matches *pattern*. The information includes descriptions of each command's options.

Options

-d

 Print a brief description of what the command does.

-m

 Print the full description of the command in a format similar
 to that of a Unix manual page.

-s

 Print brief (short) usage information.

Examples

```
$ help -s cd              Short help
cd: cd [-L|-P] [dir]

$ help true               Full help
true: true
Return a successful result.
```

---

history   Print command-line history.

```
history [count]
history [options]
```

Print commands in the history list or manage the history file. With
no options or arguments, display the history list with command
numbers. With a *count* argument, print only that many of the most
recent commands.

Options

-a

 Append new history lines (those executed since the beginning
 of the session) to the history file.

-c

 Clear the history list (remove all entries).

-d *position*

 Delete the history item at position *position*.

-n

 Read unread history lines from the history file into the history
 list.

-p *argument* …

Perform csh-style history expansion on each *argument*, printing the results to standard output. The results are not saved in the history list.

-r

Read the history file and replace the history list with its contents.

-s *argument* …

Store the *arguments* in the history list, as a single entry.

-w

Write the current history list to the history file, overwriting it entirely.

---

if
Syntax for an if-then-else statement.

```
if condition1
then commands1
[ elif condition2
  then commands2 ]

    .
    .
    .
[ else commands3 ]
fi
```

If *condition1* is met, do *commands1*; otherwise, if *condition2* is met, do *commands2*; if neither is met, do *commands3*. Conditions are often specified with the test and [[ ]] commands. See test on page 99, and [[ ]] on page 57, for a full list of conditions, and see additional Examples under : on page 56, and exit on page 74.

Examples

Insert a 0 before numbers less than 10:

```
if [ $counter -lt 10 ]
then number=0$counter
else number=$counter
fi
```

Make a directory if it doesn't exist:

```
if [ ! -d $dir ]
then
    mkdir -m 775 $dir
fi
```

---

jobs

List running or stopped jobs.

`jobs [options] [jobIDs]`

List all running or stopped jobs, or list those specified by *jobIDs*. For example, you can check whether a long compilation or text formatting job is still running. Also useful before logging out. See the section "Job Control" on page 46.

Options

-l

List job IDs and process group IDs.

-n

List only jobs whose status changed since last notification.

-p

List process group IDs only.

-r

List running jobs only.

-x *cmd*

Replace each job ID found in *cmd* with the associated process ID and then execute *cmd*.

---

kill

Send a signal to one or more jobs.

`kill [options] IDs`

Terminate each specified process *ID* or job *ID*. You must own the process or be a privileged user. This built-in is similar to the external `kill` command, but also allows symbolic job names. Stubborn processes can be killed using signal 9. See the section "Job Control" on page 46.

The command `kill -1` prints a list of the available signal names. The list varies by system architecture; for a PC-based system, it looks like this:

```
$ kill -1                    From Bash on GNU/Linux
 1) SIGHUP      2) SIGINT      3) SIGQUIT     4) SIGILL
 5) SIGTRAP     6) SIGABRT     7) SIGBUS      8) SIGFPE
 9) SIGKILL    10) SIGUSR1    11) SIGSEGV    12) SIGUSR2
13) SIGPIPE    14) SIGALRM    15) SIGTERM    16) SIGSTKFLT
17) SIGCHLD    18) SIGCONT    19) SIGSTOP    20) SIGTSTP
21) SIGTTIN    22) SIGTTOU    23) SIGURG     24) SIGXCPU
25) SIGXFSZ    26) SIGVTALRM  27) SIGPROF    28) SIGWINCH
29) SIGIO      30) SIGPWR     31) SIGSYS     34) SIGRTMIN
35) SIGRTMIN+1 36) SIGRTMIN+2 37) SIGRTMIN+3 38) SIGRTMIN+4
39) SIGRTMIN+5 40) SIGRTMIN+6 41) SIGRTMIN+7 42) SIGRTMIN+8
43) SIGRTMIN+9 44) SIGRTMIN+10 45) SIGRTMIN+11 46) SIGRTMIN+12
47) SIGRTMIN+13 48) SIGRTMIN+14 49) SIGRTMIN+15 50) SIGRTMAX-14
51) SIGRTMAX-13 52) SIGRTMAX-12 53) SIGRTMAX-11 54) SIGRTMAX-10
55) SIGRTMAX-9 56) SIGRTMAX-8 57) SIGRTMAX-7 58) SIGRTMAX-6
59) SIGRTMAX-5 60) SIGRTMAX-4 61) SIGRTMAX-3 62) SIGRTMAX-2
63) SIGRTMAX-1 64) SIGRTMAX
```

The signals and their numbers are defined in the C `<signal.h>` header file. This file may include others, thus the actual location varies across systems.

Options

`-1 [n]`

List the signal names. (Used by itself.) A numeric value *n* is interpreted as either a signal number, or as an exit status for a process terminated by a signal (128 + *n*). In both cases, `kill` prints the corresponding signal name.

`-n num`

Send the given signal number.

`-s name`

Send the given signal name.

`-signal`

The signal number (from `<signal.h>`) or name (from `kill -1`). With a signal number of 9, the kill is absolute.

---

let

```
let expressions
(( expressions ))
```

Perform arithmetic as specified by one or more *expressions*. *expressions* consist of numbers, operators, and shell variables (which don't need a preceding $). Expressions must be quoted if they contain spaces or other special characters. The (( )) form does the quoting for you. For more information and examples, see the section "Arithmetic Expressions" on page 36. See also *expr*(1).

Examples

Each of these examples adds 1 to variable i:

```
i=`expr $i + 1`        All Bourne shells
let i=i+1              Bash
let "i = i + 1"
(( i = i + 1 ))
(( i += 1 ))
(( i++ ))
```

---

local

```
local [options] [name[=value]]
```

Declares local variables for use inside functions. The *options* are the same as those accepted by declare; see declare on page 68 for the full list. It is an error to use local outside a function body.

---

logout

```
logout
```

Exit a login shell. The command fails if the current shell is not a login shell.

mapfile

Read a file into a shell array.

```
mapfile [options] [array]
```

Read standard input into *array*, one line per element. If no *array*, use MAPFILE. An alternate file descriptor may be given with the -u option.

Options

-c *count*

> Specifies the "quantum" for the -C option. The default value is 5,000.

-C *command*

> Every "quantum" lines, evaluate *command*, passing it the index in *array* that is about to be assigned. The quantum is set with the -c option.

-n *count*

> Read at most *count* lines. If *count* is zero, read all the lines.

-O *index*

> Fill *array* starting at origin *index*. The default origin is zero.

-s *count*

> Ignore the first *count* lines.

-t

> Remove the trailing newline from each line read.

-u *n*

> Read from file descriptor *n* instead of from standard input.

---

popd

Pop a directory off of the directory stack.

```
popd [-n] [+count] [-count]
```

Pop the top directory off the directory stack (as shown by the dirs command), and change to the new top directory, or manage the directory stack.

Options

-n
> Don't change to the new top directory; just manipulate the stack.

+*count*
> Remove the item *count* entries from the left, as shown by dirs. Counting starts at zero. No directory change occurs.

-*count*
> Remove the item *count* entries from the right, as shown by dirs. Counting starts at zero. No directory change occurs.

---

printf   Do formatted printing of command-line arguments.

printf [-v *var*] *format* [*val* …]

Formatted printing, like the ANSI C printf function. The format string is reused from the beginning if there are more values than format specifiers.

Option

-v *var*
> Save the result in *var* instead of printing it to standard output. *var* may be an array element.

Additional Format Letters

Bash accepts these additional format letters:

%b
> Expand escape sequences in strings (e.g., \t to tab, and so on).

%q
> Print a quoted string that can be reread later on.

pushd   **Push a directory onto the directory stack.**

```
pushd [-n] [directory]
pushd [-n] [+count] [-count]
```

Add *directory* to the directory stack, or rotate the directory stack.
With no arguments, swap the top two entries on the stack, and
change to the new top entry.

Options

-n

> Don't change to the new top directory; just manipulate the
> stack.

+*count*

> Rotate the stack so that the *count*'th item from the left, as
> shown by dirs, is the new top of the stack. Counting starts at
> zero. The new top becomes the current directory.

-*count*

> Rotate the stack so that the *count*'th item from the right, as
> shown by dirs, is the new top of the stack. Counting starts at
> zero. The new top becomes the current directory.

---

pwd   **Print working directory.**

```
pwd [-LP]
```

Print the present working directory on standard output.

Options

Options give control over the use of logical versus physical treat-
ment of the printed path. See also the entry for cd on page 62.

-L

> Use logical path (what the user typed, including any symbolic
> links) and the value of PWD for the current directory. This is the
> default.

-P

> Use the filesystem physical path for the current directory.

---

read   **Read data into one or more shell variables.**

`read [options] [variable1 [variable2 …]]`

Read one line of standard input and assign each word to the corresponding *variable*, with all leftover words assigned to the last variable. If only one variable is specified, the entire line is assigned to that variable. See the Examples here and under `case` on page 60. The return status is 0 unless *EOF* is reached. If no variables are given, input is stored in the REPLY variable.

Options

-a *array*

    Read into indexed array *array*.

-d *delim*

    Read up to the first occurrence of *delim*, instead of newline.

-e

    Use the *readline* library if reading from a terminal.

-i *text*

    When using the *readline* library, put *text* into the initial editing buffer.

-n *count*

    Read at most *count* bytes. If a delimiter character is seen before reading *count* bytes, stop reading further input.

-N *count*

    Read at most *count* bytes. Delimiter characters in the data do not cause Bash to stop reading; instead they are included in the data that is read.

-p *prompt*

    Print *prompt* before reading input.

-r

    Raw mode; ignore \ as a line-continuation character.

-s

    Read silently; characters are not echoed.

-t *timeout*

> When reading from a terminal or pipe, if no data is entered
> after *timeout* seconds, return 1. This prevents an application
> from hanging forever, waiting for user input. Values for *time-
> out* may be fractional. If *timeout* is zero but data is available to
> be read, **read** will return successfully. Partial input read when
> the *timeout* expires is saved in *variable1*; the other variables
> are cleared. **read** returns greater than 128 if no data were read
> and the *timeout* expires.

-u *[n]*

> Read input from file descriptor *n* (default is 0).

Examples

Read three variables:

```
$ read first last address
Sarah Caldwell 123 Main Street

$ echo "$last, $first\n$address"
Caldwell, Sarah
123 Main Street
```

Prompt yourself to enter two temperatures:

```
$ read -p "High low: " n1 n2
High low: 65 33
```

---

readarray   Read a file into a shell array.

```
readarray [options] [array]
```

Identical to the `mapfile` command. See `mapfile` on page 86 for more
information.

---

readonly   Mark variables as read only.

```
readonly [-afp] [variable[=value] …]
```

Prevent the specified shell variables from being assigned new values.
An initial value may be supplied using the assignment syntax, but
that value may not be changed subsequently. Read-only variables
may not be unset.

Options

`-a`

> Each *variable* must refer to an indexed array.

`-A`

> Each *variable* must refer to an associative array.

`-f`

> Each *variable* must refer to a function.

`-p`

> Print readonly before printing the names and values of read-only variables. This allows saving a list of read-only variables for rereading later.

---

return
Return an exit status from a shell function.

`return [n]`

Use inside a function definition. Exit the function with status *n* or with the exit status of the previously executed command. If *n* is negative, precede it with `--`.

---

select
Present a menu of items for use in executing a block of code.

```
select x [in list]
do
    commands
done
```

Display a list of menu items on standard error, numbered in the order they are specified in *list*. If no in *list* is given, items are taken from the command line (via `"$@"`). Following the menu is a prompt string (the value of PS3). At the $PS3 prompt, users select a menu item by typing its number, or they redisplay the menu by pressing the Enter key. User input is stored in the shell variable REPLY. If a valid item number is typed, the shell sets *x* to the chosen value and executes *commands*. Typing *EOF* terminates the loop.

Example

```
PS3="Select the item number: "
select event in Format Page View Exit
do
    case "$event" in
    Format) nroff $file | lp;;
    Page)   pr $file | lp;;
    View)   more $file;;
    Exit)   exit 0;;
    *  )    echo "Invalid selection";;
    esac
done
```

The output of this script looks like this:

```
1. Format
2. Page
3. View
4. Exit
Select the item number:
```

---

set   **Manage shell options and the script's command-line parameters.**

`set [options arg1 arg2 …]`

With no arguments, **set** prints the values of all variables known to the current shell. Options can be enabled (*-option*) or disabled (*+option*). Options can also be set when the shell is invoked. (See the section "Invoking the Shell" on page 4.) Arguments are assigned in order to $1, $2, etc.

Options

-a

    From now on, automatically mark variables for export after defining or changing them.

-b

    Print job completion messages as soon as jobs terminate; don't wait until the next prompt.

-B

    Enable brace expansion. On by default.

-C

    Prevent overwriting via > redirection; use >| to overwrite files.

-e

> Exit if a command yields a nonzero exit status. The ERR trap executes before the shell exits. The exact behavior is complicated; see "set -e Details" on page 97, later in this entry.

-E

> Cause shell functions, command substitutions, and subshells to inherit the ERR trap.

-f

> Ignore filename metacharacters (e.g., * ? [ ]).

-h

> Locate commands as they are defined. On by default. See the entry for hash on page 79.

-H

> Enable csh-style history substitution. On by default. See the section "C-Shell–Style History" on page 39.

-k

> Assignment of environment variables (*var=value*) takes effect regardless of where they appear on the command line. Normally, assignments must precede the command name.

-m

> Enable job control; background jobs execute in a separate process group. -m is usually set automatically.

-n

> Read commands but don't execute; useful for checking syntax. Interactive shells ignore this option.

+o [*mode*]

> With *mode*, disable the given shell mode. Plain set +o prints the settings of all the current modes. This is in a form that can be reread by the shell later.

-o [*mode*]

> List shell modes, or turn on mode *mode*. Many modes can be set by other options. Modes are:

> | allexport | Same as -a. |
> |---|---|
> | braceexpand | Same as -B. |

emacs	Set command-line editor to emacs.
errexit	Same as -e.
errtrace	Same as -E.
functrace	Same as -T.
hashall	Same as -h.
histexpand	Same as -H.
history	Enable command history. On by default.
ignoreeof	Don't process *EOF* signals. To exit the shell, type exit.
keyword	Same as -k.
monitor	Same as -m.
noclobber	Same as -C.
noexec	Same as -n.
noglob	Same as -f.
nolog	Omit function definitions from the history file. Accepted but ignored by Bash.
notify	Same as -b.
nounset	Same as -u.
onecmd	Same as -t.
physical	Same as -P.
pipefail	Change pipeline exit status to be that of the rightmost command that failed, or zero if all exited successfully.
posix	Change to POSIX mode.
privileged	Same as -p.
verbose	Same as -v.
vi	Set command-line editor to vi.
xtrace	Same as -x.

+p

Reset effective UID to real UID.

-p

Start up as a privileged user. Don't read $ENV or $BASH_ENV, don't import functions from the environment, and ignore the values of the BASHOPTS, CDPATH, GLOBIGNORE, and SHELLOPTS variables.

-P

Always use physical paths for cd and pwd.

-t

Exit after one command is executed.

-T

Cause shell functions, command substitutions, and subshells to inherit the DEBUG and RETURN traps.

-u

In substitutions, treat unset variables as errors. However, references to $@ and $* are not errors when there are no positional parameters.

-v

Show each shell command line when read.

-x

Show commands and arguments when executed, preceded by the value of PS4. This provides step-by-step tracing of shell scripts.

-

Turn off -v and -x, and turn off option processing. Included for compatibility with older versions of the Bourne shell.

--

Used as the last option; -- turns off option processing so that arguments beginning with - are not misinterpreted as options. (For example, you can set $1 to -1.) If no arguments are given after --, unset the positional parameters.

Option Summary

Option	Same as
-a	-o allexport
-b	-o notify
-B	-o braceexpand
-C	-o noclobber
-e	-o errexit
-E	-o errtrace

Option	Same as
-f	-o noglob
-h	-o hashall
-H	-o histexpand
-k	-o keyword
-m	-o monitor
-n	-o noexec
-o allexport	-a
-o braceexpand	-B
-o emacs	
-o errexit	-e
-o errtrace	-E
-o functrace	-T
-o hashall	-h
-o history	
-o histexpand	-H
-o ignoreeof	
-o keyword	-k
-o monitor	-m
-o noclobber	-C
-o noexec	-n
-o noglob	-f
-o nolog	
-o notify	-b
-o nounset	-u
-o onecmd	-t
-o physical	-P
-o pipefail	
-o posix	
-o privileged	-p
-o verbose	-v

Option	Same as
-o vi	
-o xtrace	-x
-p	-o privileged
-P	-o physical
-t	-o onecmd
-T	-o functrace
-u	-o nonunset
-v	-o verbose
-x	-o xtrace

set -e Details

When set -e is enabled, the shell exits if one of the following fails: a pipeline (which can be just a single command); a subshell command in parentheses; or any of the commands in a group enclosed in braces. In POSIX mode, shells created to run command substitutions inherit the setting of set -e; otherwise Bash clears the option in such subshells.

Failure of a command (non-zero exit status) does not cause an exit in the following cases: Any command in a list following while or until; the pipeline following if or elif; any command in an && or || list except the last; any command in a pipeline but the last; or if the sense of the command's value is being inverted with !.

Examples

```
set -- "$num" -20 -30      Set $1 to $num, $2 to -20, $3 to -30
set -vx                    Read each command line; show it;
                           execute it; show it again (with arguments)
set +x                     Stop command tracing
set -o noclobber           Prevent file overwriting
set +o noclobber           Allow file overwriting again
```

shift

Shift the command-line arguments left.

```
shift [n]
```

Shift positional arguments (e.g., $2 becomes $1). If *n* is given, shift to the left *n* places. Used in `while` loops to iterate through command-line arguments.

Example

```
shift $(($1 + $6))
```
Use expression result as shift count

---

shopt

Manage shell options.

```
shopt [-opqsu] [option]
```

Set or unset shell options. With no options or just -p, print the names and settings of the options. See the section "Shell Options" on page 47, for a description of the various options.

Options

-o

Each *option* must be one of the shell option names for `set -o`, instead of the options listed in "Shell Options" on page 47.

-p

Print the option settings as `shopt` commands that can be reread later.

-q

Quiet mode. The exit status is zero if the given option is set, nonzero otherwise. With multiple options, all of them must be set for a zero exit status.

-s

Set the given *options*. With no *options*, print only those that are set.

-u

Unset the given *options*. With no *options*, print only those that are unset.

source **Read and execute a file within the current shell.**

```
source file [arguments]
```

Identical to the . (dot) command; see the entry for . on page 56, for more information.

---

suspend **Suspend the current shell.**

```
suspend [-f]
```

Suspend the current shell. Often used to stop an su command.

Option

-f

    Force the suspension, even if the shell is a login shell.

---

test **Evaluate conditions, for use in loops and conditionals.**

```
test condition
[ condition ]
[[ condition ]]
```

Evaluate a *condition* and, if its value is true, return a zero exit status; otherwise, return a nonzero exit status. An alternate form of the command uses [ ] rather than the word test. An additional alternate form uses [[ ]], in which case word splitting and pathname expansion are not done (see [[ ]] on page 57). *condition* is constructed using the following expressions. Conditions are true if the description holds true.

File Conditions

-a *file*   *file* exists. (Deprecated; use -e instead.)

-b *file*   *file* exists and is a block special file.

-c *file*   *file* exists and is a character special file.

-d *file*   *file* exists and is a directory.

-e *file*   *file* exists. (Same as -a, for POSIX compatibility.)

-f *file*   *file* exists and is a regular file.

-g *file*	*file* exists, and its set-group-id bit is set.
-G *file*	*file* exists, and its group is the effective group ID.
-h *file*	*file* exists and is a symbolic link. (Same as -L.)
-k *file*	*file* exists, and its sticky bit is set.
-L *file*	*file* exists and is a symbolic link. (Same as -h.)
-N *file*	*file* exists and was modified after it was last read.
-O *file*	*file* exists, and its owner is the effective user ID.
-p *file*	*file* exists and is a named pipe (FIFO).
-r *file*	*file* exists and is readable.
-s *file*	*file* exists and has a size greater than zero.
-S *file*	*file* exists and is a socket.
-t [*n*]	The open file descriptor *n* is associated with a terminal device; default *n* is 1.
-u *file*	*file* exists, and its set-user-id bit is set.
-w *file*	*file* exists and is writable.
-x *file*	*file* exists and is executable.
f1 -ef *f2*	Files *f1* and *f2* are linked (refer to same file).
f1 -nt *f2*	File *f1* is newer than *f2*.
f1 -ot *f2*	File *f1* is older than *f2*.

String Conditions

string	*string* is not null.
-n *s1*	String *s1* has nonzero length.
-z *s1*	String *s1* has zero length.
s1 == *s2*	Strings *s1* and *s2* are identical. Inside [[ ]], *s2* can be a wildcard pattern. Quote *s2* to treat it literally. (See the section "Filename Metacharacters" on page 7. See also the nocasematch option in "Shell Options" on page 47.)
s1 = *s2*	Same as the == operator. Should be used with test and [ ] for compatibility with POSIX and other shells.
s1 != *s2*	Strings *s1* and *s2* are *not* identical. Inside [[ ]], *s2* can be a wildcard pattern. Quote *s2* to treat it literally.

s1 =~ *s2*   String *s1* matches extended regular expression *s2*. Only available inside [[ ]]. Quote *s2* to force string matching, instead of regular expression matching. Strings matched by parenthesized subexpressions are placed into elements of the BASH_REMATCH array. See the description of BASH_REMATCH in the section "Built-in Shell Variables" on page 24. See also the compat31, compat32, and compat40 options in "Shell Options" on page 47.

s1 < *s2*   String value of *s1* precedes that of *s2*. Bash uses the locale's sorting order. (Use only within [[ ]].)

s1 > *s2*   String value of *s1* follows that of *s2*. Bash uses the locale's sorting order. (Use only within [[ ]].)

Internal Shell Conditions

-o *opt*   Option *opt* for set -o is on.

Integer Comparisons

n1 -eq *n2*   *n1* equals *n2*.

n1 -ge *n2*   *n1* is greater than or equal to *n2*.

n1 -gt *n2*   *n1* is greater than *n2*.

n1 -le *n2*   *n1* is less than or equal to *n2*.

n1 -lt *n2*   *n1* is less than *n2*.

n1 -ne *n2*   *n1* does not equal *n2*.

Combined Forms

(*condition*)
> True if *condition* is true (used for grouping). For test and [ ], the parentheses should be quoted by a \. The form using [[ ]] doesn't require quoting the parentheses.

! *condition*
> True if *condition* is false.

condition1 -a *condition2*
> True if both conditions are true.

condition1 && *condition2*
> True if both conditions are true. Short-circuit form. (Use only within [[ ]].)

condition1 -o *condition2*
> True if either condition is true.

condition1 || *condition2*
> True if either condition is true. Short-circuit form. (Use only within [[ ]].)

Examples

The following examples show the first line of various statements that might use a test condition:

```
while test $# -gt 0          While there are arguments
while [ -n "$1" ]            While there are nonempty arguments
if [ $count -lt 10 ]         If $count is less than 10
if [ -d RCS ]                If the RCS directory exists
if [ "$answer" != "y" ]      If the answer is not y
if [ ! -r "$1" -o ! -f "$1" ]  If the first argument is not a
                             readable file or a regular file
```

---

time   Time a command.

`time` *command*

Execute *command* and print the total elapsed time, user time, and system time (in seconds). Same as the external command `time`, except that the built-in version can also time other built-in commands as well as all commands in a pipeline.

---

times   Print accumulated CPU times.

`times`

Print accumulated process times for user and system.

---

trap   Manage the disposition of signals within a shell script.

```
trap [ [commands] signals]
trap -p
trap -l
```

Execute *commands* if any *signals* are received. The second form prints the current trap settings in a form suitable for rereading later. The third form lists all signals and their numbers, like `kill -l`.

Common signals include EXIT (0), HUP (1), INT (2), and TERM (15). Multiple commands must be quoted as a group and separated by semicolons internally. If *commands* is the null string (i.e., `trap ""` *signals*), *signals* are ignored by the shell. If *commands* are omitted entirely, reset processing of specified signals to the default action. If *commands* is "-", reset *signals* to their initial defaults.

In general, *commands* should be quoted using single quotes, so that any variable or other substitutions are delayed until the signal is handled. Otherwise, with double quotes, the expansions would be evaluated earlier, when the **trap** command itself is executed.

If both *commands* and *signals* are omitted, list current trap assignments. See the Examples here and in exec on page 74.

Signals

A list of signal names, numbers, and meanings were given in the entry for `kill` on page 83. The shell allows you to use either the signal number or the signal name (without the SIG prefix). In addition, the shell supports "pseudo-signals," signal names or numbers that aren't real operating system signals but which direct the shell to perform a specific action. These signals are:

DEBUG	Execution of any command.
ERR	Nonzero exit status.
EXIT	Exit from shell (usually when shell script finishes).
RETURN	A `return` is executed, or a script run with `.` (dot) or `source` finishes.
0	Same as EXIT, for historical compatibility with the Bourne shell.

Examples

```
trap "" INT        Ignore interrupts (signal 2)
trap INT           Obey interrupts again
```

Remove a $tmp file when the shell program exits, or if the user logs out, presses CTRL-C, or does a kill:

```
trap "rm -f $tmp; exit" EXIT HUP INT TERM POSIX style
trap "rm -f $tmp; exit" 0 1 2 15        Original Bourne shell
```

Print a "clean up" message when the shell program receives signals SIGHUP, SIGINT, or SIGTERM:

```
trap 'echo Interrupt!  Cleaning up…' HUP INT TERM
```

---

true   Exit with a true return value.

true

Built-in command that exits with a true return value.

---

type   Print the type of a command.

type [-afpPt] commands

Show whether each command name is an external command, a built-in command, an alias, a shell keyword, or a defined shell function.

Options

-a

> Print all locations in $PATH that include *command*, including aliases and functions. Use -p together with -a to suppress aliases and functions.

-f

> Suppress function lookup, as with command.

-p

> If type -t would print file for a given *command*, print the full pathname for the corresponding executable files. Otherwise, print nothing.

-P

> Like -p, but force a search of $PATH, even if type -t would not print file.

-t

> Print a word describing each *command*. The word is one of alias, builtin, file, function, or keyword, depending upon the type of each *command*.

Example

```
$ type mv read if
mv is /bin/mv
read is a shell builtin
if is a shell keyword
```

---

typeset   Declare shell variables and manage their attributes.

typeset [*options*] [*variable*[=*value* …]]

Identical to declare. See the entry for declare on page 68.

---

ulimit   Manage various process limits.

ulimit [*options*] [*n*]

Print the value of one or more resource limits, or, if *n* is specified, set a resource limit to *n*. Resource limits can be either hard (-H) or soft (-S). By default, ulimit sets both limits or prints the soft limit. The options determine which resource is acted upon.

Options

-H

> Hard limit. Anyone can lower a hard limit; only privileged users can raise it.

-S

> Soft limit. Must be less than or equal to the hard limit.

-a

> Print all limits.

`-b`

Maximum size of a socket buffer.

`-c`

Maximum size of core files. Default units are 1K-byte blocks. In POSIX mode, units are 512-byte blocks.

`-d`

Maximum kilobytes of data segment or heap.

`-e`

Maximum scheduling priority (nice value).

`-f`

Maximum size of files (the default option). Default units are 1K-byte blocks. In POSIX mode, units are 512-byte blocks.

`-i`

Maximum number of pending signals.

`-l`

Maximum size of address space that can be locked in memory.

`-m`

Maximum kilobytes of physical memory. (Not effective on all Unix systems.)

`-n`

Maximum number of file descriptors.

`-p`

Size of pipe buffers. (Not effective on all Unix systems.)

`-q`

Maximum number of bytes in POSIX message queues.

`-r`

Maximum real-time scheduling priority.

`-s`

Maximum kilobytes of stack segment.

`-t`

Maximum CPU seconds.

`-T`

Maximum number of threads.

-u

    Maximum number of processes a single user can have.

-v

    Maximum kilobytes of virtual memory. (Not effective on all Unix systems.)

-x

    Maximum number of file locks.

---

umask   Display or set the process's file creation mask.

```
umask [nnn]
umask [-pS] [mask]
```

Display file creation mask or set file creation mask to octal value *nnn*. The file creation mask determines which permission bits are turned off (e.g., umask 002 produces rw-rw-r--). For the second form, a symbolic mask represents permissions to keep.

Options

-p

    Output is in a form that can be reread later by the shell.

-S

    Print the current mask using symbolic notation.

---

unalias   Remove previously defined aliases.

```
unalias names
unalias -a
```

Remove *names* from the alias list. See also `alias` on page 58.

Option

-a

    Remove all aliases.

unset

Remove variables or functions.

unset [*options*] *names*

Erase definitions of functions or variables listed in *names*.

Options

-f

> Unset functions *names*.

-v

> Unset variables *names* (default).

---

until

Syntax for a loop that runs until a condition becomes true.

```
until condition
do
    commands
done
```

Until *condition* is met, do *commands*. *condition* is often specified with the test command. See the Examples under case on page 60, and test on page 99.

---

wait

Wait for a process or job to complete.

wait [*ID*]

With no *ID*, pause in execution until all background jobs complete (exit status 0 is returned), or pause until the specified background process *ID* or job *ID* completes (exit status of *ID* is returned). Note that the shell variable $! contains the process ID of the most recent background process.

Example

> wait $!   *Wait for most recent background process to finish*

while   Syntax for a loop that runs while a condition remains true.

```
while condition
do
    commands
done
```

While *condition* is met, do *commands*. *condition* is often specified with the test command. See the Examples under case on page 60, and test on page 99.

---

filename   Run an external command.

```
filename [arguments]
```

Read and execute commands from executable file *filename*, or execute a binary object file.

Resources

This section briefly describes other sources of information about Bash.

Online Resources

http://ftp.gnu.org/gnu/bash
> The top-level directory for Bash source code releases. Source code is usually made available as .tar.gz files, such as bash-4.1.tar.gz.

ftp://ftp.gnu.org/pub/gnu/bash/bash-4.1-patches
> Patches for Bash 4.1 are in this directory.

http://www.gnu.org/software/bash/bash.html, *http://tiswww.tis .cwru.edu/~chet/bash/bashtop.html*
> The two "home pages" for the Bash shell.

http://bashdb.sourceforge.net
> The Bash debugger.

http://freshmeat.net/projects/bashcompletion
> Ian Macdonald's collected set of completion specifications.

http://www.opengroup.org/onlinepubs/009695399
> The online version of the POSIX standard.

Books

Newham, Cameron. *Learning the bash Shell*, Third Edition. Sebastopol: O'Reilly Media, 2005.

Robbins, Arnold, and Nelson H.F. Beebe. *Classic Shell Scripting*. Sebastopol: O'Reilly Media, 2005.

Acknowledgments

Thanks to Chet Ramey, the Bash maintainer, for providing access to early releases of Bash 4.1, and for once again reviewing this reference. Thanks to Robert P.J. Day for reviewing this edition. Thanks again to Mike Loukides at O'Reilly Media for his continued support of this project.

Index

Symbols

! (exclamation mark)
  != inequality operator, 37
  event designators, 40
  filename metacharacter, 7
  logical negation operator, 36
" (quotation marks, double)
  " " quoting, 10
  escape sequence, 11
(hash mark), comments, 10, 55
#!shell command, 56
$ (dollar sign)
  $( ) command substitution, 12
  $(( )) arithmetic substitution, 12
  ${ } variable substitution, 21
  last argument, 40
  shell variables, 24
  variable substitution, 10
$ENV file (read by Bash shell at startup), 6
% (percent)
  argument matched by, 40
  job control, 46
  modulus operator, 36
& (ampersand)
  && logical AND operator, 57
  background execution, 10
  bitwise AND operator, 37
  logical AND operator, 37
' (quotation marks, single)
  escape sequence, 11
  quoting, 10
() (parentheses), command grouping, 10
* (asterisk)
  ** exponentiation operator, 36
  ** filename metacharacters, 7

We'd like to hear your suggestions for improving our indexes. Send email to *index@oreilly.com*.

Get even more for your money.

Join the O'Reilly Community, and register the O'Reilly books you own. It's free, and you'll get:

- $4.99 ebook upgrade offer
- 40% upgrade offer on O'Reilly print books
- Membership discounts on books and events
- Free lifetime updates to ebooks and videos
- Multiple ebook formats, DRM FREE
- Participation in the O'Reilly community
- Newsletters
- Account management
- 100% Satisfaction Guarantee

Registering your books is easy:
1. Go to: oreilly.com/go/register
2. Create an O'Reilly login.
3. Provide your address.
4. Register your books.

Note: English-language books only

To order books online:
oreilly.com/store

For questions about products or an order:
orders@oreilly.com

To sign up to get topic-specific email announcements and/or news about upcoming books, conferences, special offers, and new technologies:
elists@oreilly.com

For technical questions about book content:
booktech@oreilly.com

To submit new book proposals to our editors:
proposals@oreilly.com

O'Reilly books are available in multiple DRM-free ebook formats. For more information:
oreilly.com/ebooks

O'REILLY®

Spreading the knowledge of innovators | oreilly.com

The information you need, when and where you need it.

With Safari Books Online, you can:

Access the contents of thousands of technology and business books

- Quickly search over 7000 books and certification guides
- Download whole books or chapters in PDF format, at no extra cost, to print or read on the go
- Copy and paste code
- Save up to 35% on O'Reilly print books
- **New!** Access mobile-friendly books directly from cell phones and mobile devices

Stay up-to-date on emerging topics before the books are published

- Get on-demand access to evolving manuscripts.
- Interact directly with authors of upcoming books

Explore thousands of hours of video on technology and design topics

- Learn from expert video tutorials
- Watch and replay recorded conference sessions

O'REILLY®